FOLLOWING
IN THE FOOTSTEPS
OF ABRAHAM

FOLLOWING
IN THE FOOTSTEPS
OF ABRAHAM

SERMONS BY
JOHN DOUGLAS

EDITED AND ARRANGED BY
SARA ELLIOTT

AMBASSADOR

Belfast Northern Ireland Greenville South Carolina

FOLLOWING IN THE FOOTSTEPS OF ABRAHAM

ISBN 1 84030 072 8

*With special thanks to
Gene Elliott, Carolyn McNeely
and Chad Mitchel
for their invaluable assistance*

Ambassador Publications
a division of
Ambassador Productions Ltd.
Providence House
16 Hillview Avenue,
Belfast, BT5 6JR
Northern Ireland
www.ambassador-productions.com

Emerald House
1 Chick Springs Road, Suite 203
Greenville,
South Carolina 29609, USA
www.emeraldhouse.com

CONTENTS

ABRAHAM

the consummate pilgrim, the disciple of Christ, shows us how to walk the Christian pathway. Begin with this venerable patriarch as he leaves his homeland, and follow him to Moriah's Hill. Learn with Abraham that the pitfalls are many, but the rewards are eternal, and that all who know the Saviour must traverse this road.

CHAPTER ONE

BY FAITH - ABRAHAM'S IDENTITY

❚❚ By faith Abraham, when he was called to go out into a place which he should after receive for an inheritance, obeyed ... By faith he sojourned in the land of promise ... By faith Abraham, when he was tried, offered up Isaac: and he that had received the promises offered up his only begotten son. ❚❚

Hebrews 11:8-19

*❚❚ For what saith the scripture? Abraham believed God, and it was counted unto him for righteousness ... And he received the sign of circumcision, a seal of the righteousness of the faith which he had yet being uncircumcised: **that he might be the father of all them that believe** ... Therefore it is of faith, that it might be by grace; to the end the promise might be sure*

to all the seed; not to that only which is of the law, but to
that also which is of the faith of Abraham; who is the
father of us all ... He staggered not at the promise of God
through unbelief; but was strong in faith, giving glory to
God; And being fully persuaded that, what he had
promised, he was able also to perform. **//**

Romans 4:3-21

IN THE BOOK OF GENESIS, the beginning of God's written
revelation that spans twenty-three hundred years in its fifty
chapters, our attention is drawn to an arresting figure—the
man Abraham. Though he shares centre stage with other great
men such as Adam, Noah, Jacob, and Joseph, we can see that
God has placed definite emphasis on the vital details of
Abraham's life.

A bird's-eye view of Genesis reveals that this book falls
into two distinct parts: chapters 1 to 11, and chapters 12 to the
end. In these chapters we read the life stories of a number of
different people, but the five characters mentioned above
dominate. Of those five, Abraham stands in the middle
chronologically, and in the key place by virtue of the number
of chapters given to his story.

The account of Abraham's life belongs to the second and
major part of the book—chapters 12 to 25. Abraham lived 175
years; one hundred of those years are given mention in the
Scripture. It is significant that these hundred years occupy
fourteen chapters of Genesis, while twenty-two hundred years
occupy the remaining thirty-six chapters. The Holy Spirit
relates the events of the Creation week in Genesis chapter 1.
Then chapters 2 to 6 cover about two thousand years. But in
chapters 12 to 25, time suddenly slows down, and we see *one*
hundred years of one man's life. You have to say that this period
of years must be very, very significant in the eyes of the

Lord. Certainly, God is telling us that we must take note of Abraham!

The importance of Abraham's life.

Though great attention is given to Abraham's account, God does not begin to deal with his life until Abraham is seventy-five years old. This is astonishing! What do we know of Abraham when he was twenty-five, just a young man? Nothing. What do we know of Abraham when he was forty? We have not a detail to record. Passing over the first seventy-five years of Abraham's life in virtual silence, God shows us that when He does not work in a person's life, those years are wasted. He would have us know that the years of our lives not spent in recognition of the Lord, not spent in prayerful dedication to the Lord, are really lost years. I wonder, when we all stand before the Lord at the judgment seat of Christ, how many years of our lives will be null and void? How many of us will weep and lament over wasted years?

The fact that this great patriarch's walk with God did not begin until later life, gives us cause for encouragement as well. Some of us who have reached our golden years may be tempted to feel that the best of our lives is behind us. That might be true physically, but it does not have to be true spiritually. God has a ministry not only for the young, but for the old also. Consider the scene when the Saviour as a babe was brought into the temple. Where were all the young people? We are struck to discover two ancient saints, an old man ready to die, and a woman well into the years of seniority. To the old, I say that this could be a key time in your life when the Lord will begin to work in your own soul in a way that you have not experienced before. Abraham was seventy-five when he entered into Canaan, when he got into victory, seventy-five when he entered into blessing, seventy-five when he started to obey to the fullness of his ability. He was an old man, yet one of the most important men in all of Scripture.

The prominence of Abraham in Hebrews 11.

Further proof of Abraham's importance comes in the New Testament commentary on the people of faith. Hebrews 11 mentions fourteen leading servants of God. God gives one verse each to the description of Noah, Enoch, and Abel. Certainly, a man like Noah could have more details of his life and experience with God presented in this chapter, but the Holy Spirit limits the commentary to just one verse. And how valuable would be a detailing of events in Enoch's life, for he walked with God. He must have had remarkable experiences with the Lord, but God summarizes them in one verse. There is Abel, who pictured the Shepherd Saviour. We would love to know more about him, but we have only one verse. Then we come to the commentary on Abraham's faith. He has *twelve verses* to himself, nearly as much as the rest of the people mentioned in Hebrews 11 put together! We have to say that God intends us to watch this man. If we are going to study one of the biographies in the book of Genesis, we could not take a better one than that of Abraham.

Who was Abraham? Historically, he was a Semite, born about 2166 B.C. into a pagan family living in the land of Ur in Babylonia. Leaving his home at the age of seventy-five, Abraham entered Canaan. He was about eighty when he talked with Melchizedek. His first son, Ishmael, was born when he was eighty-six. He saw the judgment of the city of Sodom when he was ninety-nine. Isaac was born when Abraham was one hundred years old, and Sarah was buried when he was 137. His death came at 175 years of age, 115 years before Jacob and his family went into Egypt.

Why study Abraham?

But what of all that? Why do we consider the study of this man's life so beneficial to our Christian walk? Primarily for two reasons: because it was through Abraham and his descendants that God chose to mediate the covenant blessings; and because Abraham demonstrated a pattern for every faithful believer walking the path of obedience to the Saviour.

Much of the story of redemption began with Abraham. That story, barely outlined in the Garden of Eden, now four hundred years after the Deluge, was to continue with the call of the father of a chosen people who would manifest God's saving grace. Abraham—the man of faith, the disciple of the Lord, the one who viewed in person from north to south, the land God promised him—was persuaded as to the existence of the heavenly city to which he would travel with all the saints. Abraham, the man of obedience, came to a high point of crisis at the sacrificial altar with Isaac his son; Isaac was the type through which Abraham learned of things to come.

Four striking cameos of Abraham's spiritual experience.

Because of his timeless message to us, we no longer ask, "Who *was* Abraham," but we ask, "Who *is* Abraham?"

1. *He is a man who left all for Jesus.* He saw Christ's day in many ways and was glad. But what did Abraham have to give up for the Lord? This venerable servant of the Lord turned his back on his homeland never to return. He departed from his father's grave, struggled to leave Lot, and gave up Ishmael. Even Eliezer had to be eliminated in the making of his faith. It was his response to the final demand of discipleship which saw him place his beloved Isaac on that altar on Moriah's heights, marking out, centuries before the time, the hill called Calvary. That experience outshines all other experiences as the grand climax of his spiritual pilgrimage.

2. *He is a man who is identified with the Land.* There is no other land like the Land of Promise, for it is the land of

Israel, the land of the Bible, and the land where Jesus walked. According to the account in Genesis 15, Abraham believed God would *give* him, in the fullness of time, that land for a personal possession, although the Scriptures reveal that he was to die first without ever having received it. The only piece of it he ever owned was the grave he lay in, and he had to *buy* that before he could have it.

3.   *He is the spiritual father of the whole family of God's redeemed.* The church, therefore, in the New Testament period, should not be viewed as a separate entity, disparate from Abraham. Rather, the epistle to the Romans, arguably the theological foundation to the New Testament Scriptures, proclaims seven times over in one chapter that Abraham is father of all who are justified by faith in Jesus. This means that there is one integral and indivisible family gathered under one head (Romans 4:1,ff.; Galatians 3:7, 8, 29). This one family consists of all God's people, irrespective of the times in which they lived.

4.   *He is a pilgrim travelling to the New Jerusalem.* The earthly inheritance is, for him and for us, the *type* of the heavenly. Places in the land and experiences in his life are a constant and powerful reminder of that which is eternal. Abraham's interest in the heavenly is not eclipsed by his commitment to the earthly. While Abraham is always the pilgrim, the stalwart follower of the Lord in the land, he is ever looking for the fulfilment of the Sacred Word. He is ever looking for the oncoming Day of Christ, the day that made him glad. *For he looked for a city which hath foundations, whose builder and maker is God* (Hebrews 11:10).

We can see that Abraham's story is a significant one for every Christian who seeks to know more of God's will. I have no doubt in my mind that if we prayerfully study the testimony of Abraham, disciple and follower of Christ, God will apply the Word to our own souls and lead us gently, lovingly, yet I pray powerfully, into a closer walk with the Lord, as we find ourselves *Following in the Footsteps of Abraham.*

CHAPTER TWO

OUT OF THY COUNTRY - ABRAHAM'S CALL

" Now the LORD had said unto Abram, Get thee out of thy country, and from thy kindred, and from thy father's house, unto a land that I will shew thee: And I will make of thee a great nation, and I will bless thee, and make thy name great: and thou shalt be a blessing: And I will bless them that bless thee, and curse him that curseth thee: and in thee shall all families of the earth be blessed. "

Genesis 12:1-3

GOD CALLS MEN. HE CALLS them to the way of life and salvation. We label that the Gospel call. God also calls His own people. He calls them into the life of full surrender and discipleship. This is the call which brought Abraham out of Ur of the Chaldees, and it is that ensuing life and walk of Abraham which, God willing, will capture our attention. For a little season we will be privileged to walk in the footsteps of Abraham, the venerable patriarch, the friend of God, the father of the faithful, the disciple of Christ, the stalwart in prayer, and according to the New Testament, the outstanding man of faith. These are but some of the titles that we can draw from the Scriptures and relate to this giant of a man who knew God. With these things in mind about Abraham, we have much to learn, and my prayer is that the Lord will be pleased to enlighten us and warm our hearts and make us to know that He Who is the God of Abraham is still with His saints.

The three-fold call of God to Abraham.

Genesis 12:1-3 has become the key passage in the study of Abraham's life. I would suggest that you take these words and think of them in relation to yourself, that you might even now pray humbly, reverently, but expectantly, and say, "Lord, open this Word to me in my own soul." Everything in the life of Abraham looks back to these words; everything else in the remainder of the book of Genesis looks back to these words; in fact, in some sense, everything else in the Bible looks back to this pivotal moment recorded in Genesis 12.

A careful look at the words of God's call clearly shows us that God called Abraham to separate himself in a threefold fashion: *Now the LORD had said unto Abram,* first, *Get thee out of thy country;* second, *from thy kindred;* third, *from thy father's house.* It was a giant step for Abraham to act upon such a word, to leave his country, to forsake his own kindred, to leave his father's house. Is it not clear that the Lord is already beginning to lay down the foundations of discipleship here? Abraham is not only a pilgrim bound for Zion, but he is a follower of Christ, that is, one who leaves all for Jesus' sake. This is discipleship. *Get thee out of thy country, from thy kindred, and from thy father's house.* It is not just a change of country that God has in mind, but Abraham must learn to leave *all* for the Saviour's sake.

The New Testament commentary on discipleship leaves us no doubt as to what God expects. Matthew 10:37 says, *He that loveth father or mother more than me is not worthy of me: and he that loveth son or daughter more than me is not worthy of me. And he that taketh not his cross, and followeth after me, is not worthy of me. He that findeth his life shall lose it: and he that loseth his life for my sake shall find it.* This passage states for us **the essence of discipleship—leaving all for Jesus.** More and more as we prayerfully look into the Scriptures and look to the Lord to work in our hearts, I do believe the Holy Spirit will show us the real meaning of discipleship. The Lord may be prompting you to turn your back on something for His name's sake. Abraham had to turn from that which was wrong. Then came the time when Abraham had to turn from that which was acceptable and proper and expected in order to be the disciple of Christ, in order that he might learn by experience to put the Saviour first. Certainly, Luke 14:33 would place the final seal on the meaning of discipleship: *So likewise, whosoever he be of you that forsaketh not all that he hath, he cannot be my disciple.*

In looking at this three-fold command God gave to Abraham, can we see all that the Lord is doing in this case? Well, certainly, He is fulfilling more purposes than one. Clearly, God is working in other situations and in other lives while He is dealing with Abraham. We often have a simplistic, one-dimensional view as we consider incidents in the Bible. We tend to be able to see just one thing which the Lord is doing, but I am convinced that **the Lord never does just a single work at a time.** I am convinced that as we peer into this story, we will see that the Lord was doing several things all at the one time. God has a definite purpose in bringing Abraham to Canaan; however, the secondary import of all that Abraham is passing through, is that God is teaching him, and all who follow in his footsteps, a powerful lesson on discipleship.

Abraham learns of the Lord Jesus.

Some Christians who hold to the dispensational view of Scripture would have difficulty in seeing that Abraham is a disciple of Christ. A few of that persuasion believe that the

Old Testament saints were saved in a different way from the rest of us, that is, that they were saved by believing in God and also by doing certain good works. This same band of believers would have you imagine that Old Testament saints knew nothing—or virtually nothing—of the Lord Jesus Christ. This is far from the truth. I say without hesitation, that when Abraham gets the call of God in far away Ur of the Chaldees, when he pulls up the tent cords and packs up his belongings, he is leaving all for Jesus' sake. Scripture teaches this fact. The Lord Jesus Christ testified to this fact when He declared in John 8:56, *Your father Abraham rejoiced to see my day: and he saw it, and was glad.* Abraham knew about the Saviour. Abraham, following the Lord in discipleship when he left all, when he turned his back on everything, did it for Jesus' sake. The Saviour certainly said that Abraham rejoiced to see His day. Then the verse emphasizes, *he saw it.* He saw clearly the Day of Christ. He saw something of the sufferings of Christ. He saw something of the glory of Christ that should be revealed at the Saviour's return in the clouds of Heaven. *Your father Abraham rejoiced to see my day: and he saw it, and was glad.* Clearly, when Abraham left all, he left all with Jesus Christ in mind.

Jesus, I my cross have taken,
All to leave and follow Thee;
Destitute, despised, forsaken,
Thou, from hence, my all shalt be:
Perish every fond ambition,
All I've sought, and hoped, and known;
Yet how rich is my condition,
God and heaven are still my own!

Haste thee on from grace to glory,
Armed by faith and winged by prayer;
Heaven's eternal day's before thee,
God's own hand shall guide thee there.
Soon shall close thy earthly mission,
Swift shall pass thy pilgrim days,
Hope shall change to glad fruition,
Faith to sight, and prayer to praise.

Abraham had to get out of Babylon.

Further, as we noted before, when God said, "Abraham, get out of this country," the Lord was fulfilling more purposes than one. In addition to teaching Abraham how to be a disciple of Jesus Christ, God would also deal with his pilgrimage to the Land of Promise. But in between all of that, God had another purpose, that of drawing this man out of a wicked environment. There was good reason for Abraham to leave the country where he had lived in his early days. Jeremiah 50:38 gives us a vivid picture of the spiritual declension of Babylon: *A drought is upon her waters; and they shall be dried up: for it is the land of graven images, and they are mad upon their idols.* It was good for Abraham himself to get out of Babylon, for according to Jeremiah, the citizens of Babylon were *mad upon their idols.* It is difficult to imagine the depth of wickedness in that horrible place. The idolatry of pagan society in days of old was no little thing. It was anguish, cruelty, darkness, horror—a nightmare we would not even want to describe.

Today, we have just no idea what it is like for a country to be "mad" about its idols, but we do see how many around us "go mad" after the things of the world. We can see people mad about this or that, not giving due attention to the Lord. For example, some of us are mad about motorbikes. It is not a sin to be interested in a motorbike, or to love riding it, or looking after it either, but you could be mad about bikes to such a degree that your spiritual witness is suffering. You could be so mad about motorbikes, or business, or any other thing, that you are losing out with God. A person who is "mad" about something is completely consumed, captivated, and motivated by that thing. It is first in his life. Now Babylon was mad about idols, but God's will for Abraham held forth for him something far, far better than that. Don't ever imagine that the Lord is a disappointment. The Lord is no disappointment. He can do better for you than the world can do. **You must learn to put the Saviour first.** This is a fact in the life of the Christian.

The strange place called Ur of the Chaldees.

It is interesting to notice that Abraham lived in the vicinity of Ur of the Chaldees. Ur is derived from a word which means *light*. Now consider Babylonish religion. Consider a land where the people were mad about their idols. This region of that whole territory was called light. The light of Babylon was there. Ur of the Chaldees was the religious capital of Babylonia, the place where the apostasy was at its worst. *If the light that is in thee be darkness, the Saviour said, how great is that darkness!* For the citizens of Babylon, Ur was the central place, their "Mecca." This was, to them, the place where men could find their way to God, but in reality it was an abomination from start to finish. It was a place of horrible darkness. God said, "Abraham, get out of this place as quickly as you can." And Abraham went out—by faith. Hebrews 11:8 tells us, *By faith Abraham, when he was called to go out into a place which he should after receive for an inheritance, obeyed; and he went out, not knowing whither he went.* Praise God for a man whose faith was such that he was content to take God's Word for it. Even though he did not know where he was going, he was convinced that God knew, and so he went out by faith.

I would say to you that if the Lord gives you counsel, if the Lord gives you direction, and He says clearly, "This is the way in which you are to go," **you can go on with God confidently, even though you cannot see into tomorrow,** even though you may not know where you are going. Abraham, such a giant as Abraham, had to say that he did not know where he was going; but for a fact, for an absolute fact, the Lord knew. This is the commentary in the New Testament by the Holy Spirit on Abraham's discipleship: he was called to go, and when he got the call to go, he went. When God spoke to him and told him to go forth, Abraham obeyed even though the way ahead was dark so that he could not see where the next step would take him. I feel convicted to say that many a time we do not trust the Lord. We say that we believe the Book from cover to cover and would not apologize for it; yet we fail to trust in the Lord enough to follow His commands and leadings, with the result that we do not honour Him as we should.

The need for patience when seeking guidance.

This same verse in Hebrews will teach us a most important truth about guidance from the Lord. **Guidance is gradual.** Very often, if not all the time, when the Lord is leading you forth, you do not see the end from the beginning. The Lord shows you only a little glimmering at a time. He will show you only enough to enable you to take the first step. Oh, don't expect to see the whole journey and don't demand of the Lord that you know everything at the start. The first step is all you need to consider. *Abraham. . . went out, not knowing whither he went.* He could see the first few steps ahead, but as for the rest of the way, he could not discern it. He trusted the Lord with it.

Is there some emptiness in your life? Is there some journey that you have to take, some commitment that you have to make and you don't see the end from the beginning? Are you faltering and holding back on God? Well, the time has come for you to seek His face and get the mind of God on it; and if the Lord seems to say to you, "Go on," even though you are faltering and hesitating, be content to **trust God with every step you take.** The Lord knows the way through the wilderness. Praise His Name!

What tho' the way be lonely
And dark the shadows fall;
I know where'er it leadeth,
My Father planned it all.

He guides my falt'ring footsteps
Along the weary way,
For well He knows the pathway
Will lead to endless day.

I sing thro' the shade and the sunshine,
I'll trust Him whatever befall;
I sing for I cannot be silent—
My Father planned it all.

Why God kept the land of Israel in mind.

Now I would like us to consider Hebrews 11:8 in the light
of Genesis 12:1. I have something very, very significant to tell
you. Abraham did not know where he was going. He had
never seen the land of Canaan before, though he might have
heard of it. I have said that the Lord knows the way through
the wilderness. The Lord *did* know the way, for Genesis 12:1 is
to be read like this—follow it carefully—*Now the LORD had*
said unto Abram, Get thee out of thy country, and from thy kindred,
and from thy father's house, unto a land that I will shew thee. Look
at that last line again: unto a land that I will shew thee. In the
Hebrew Bible, the word land has the definite article. It makes
all the difference. Get thee…unto the land that I will shew
thee. This examination of the original language shows us that
God had a definite place in mind. What a wonderful thought!
Furthermore, Deuteronomy 32:8 proves this great fact. This
chapter records the last sermon of Moses. At 120 years of age,
this great stalwart of faith, this unequalled servant of God,
Moses, comes to talk about the land of Canaan. Verse 8 says,
When the most High divided to the nations their inheritance, when
he separated the sons of Adam, he set the bounds of the people
according to the number of the children of Israel. Now when we
go back to the days of Adam, we go a long way back into
history. We are going back to the initial Creation. We are going
back to the very time when our first father as the crowning
specimen of God's Creation, lived and breathed. There in the
days of Adam, when the Lord had in mind the separation of
the earth among the sons of men, *he set the bounds of the people*
according to the number of the children of Israel. That statement
means, if it means anything, that God allocated the territories
of the earth to the respective nations, all around the land of

Israel. He had the land of Israel in mind, Israel as a people, and certainly Israel as a country. The land of Israel was already in the mind of God when Adam stood in Eden's garden. We can echo the words of Scripture which say, *Known unto God are all his works from the beginning of the world* (Acts 15:18).

Let us go on to consider Ezekiel 5:5. *Thus saith the Lord GOD; This is Jerusalem: I have set it in the midst of the nations and countries that are round about her.* Putting these pieces of information together, I am learning that when Adam stood in Paradise, in the Eden of God, already the Lord had the population of the earth in mind. The earth would be divided into nations, and in that allocation of territory to the various nations, God would determine their bounds in accordance with the placement of Israel. He would set Israel *in the midst of the nations,* for Ezekiel 5:5 says Jerusalem is set in the midst of the nations and countries that are round about her. Do I need to tell you the rest? Do I need to remind you that there is a hill outside the city wall? The God Who fashioned the mountains made that little hill called Calvary, which in time, would be outside the city wall. What do you think was in the mind of God when He fashioned that hill, when He shaped its contours, when He put it exactly where it stood on the earth and where it still stands to this day? Now my Bible tells me that all around the city of Jerusalem God put mountains—the Mount of Olivet, the best known, and other mountains—all of which can be seen to the present day. Then out there on a wing to the north, God placed that little hill called Calvary. God put it there in the midst of the nations. And when God called Abraham out of faraway Babylon, He had Israel in mind. He had redemption in mind. He would show him the country; and before the life of Abraham was through, God intended to show Abraham the very place where the Cross would be lifted up, where that final sacrifice for sin would be made once and for all. Abraham, the Scriptures say later, saw the place. *Your father Abraham rejoiced to see my day: and he saw it, and was glad.* He learned, with a thrill in his own soul that words could never describe, that the Lord would accomplish the great scheme of redemption on that hill which today stands outside the city wall.

Abraham did not go the whole way with God at the first.

Sadly, in the middle of this wonderful thought, we will have to consider another aspect of Abraham's life—that of his disobedience. It is a fact that as God speaks, we do not always hear. It is a fact that as God calls, we sometimes give only partial response. As we look at Abraham's experience, it seems, on the one hand, that Abraham is holding back; we will look at that. Then, as we move on in this study, we will see Abraham erring in the other direction and going too far. **The Christian pathway is a narrow pathway.** It is easy to go into Bypath Meadow to the right, or to fall into the Slough of Despond to the left; but it is God's will for us neither to turn to the right nor to the left, but to head straight on. In the case before us, Abraham went only halfway. Genesis 11 tells us that he got as far as Haran, and then he stopped there. Also, he brought his father with him. Actually, the Scriptures say in Genesis 11:31, *And Terah took Abram his son*   (Imagine that!) *and Lot the son of Haran his son's son.* This was in obvious disobedience to the command of the Lord, for He had said, "Abraham, leave the country, leave your kindred, and leave your father's house." But the old man came too. The Scripture actually says that Terah took Abram! At the very least, if Abraham had gone through in total obedience, it might have read, "Abram took Terah." We might at least have expected that, but it was not so, according to the Scripture's account.

It often happens that we are not long in the way of discipleship before other interests emerge and take precedence. Some of you—oh, I have to say this—can well remember from years ago the time when you laid your all on the altar. You may, even with tears, have cried to God as with burning earnestness you committed all to the Saviour's love and grace. You meant then to go the whole way with the Lord, but maybe like Abraham, other interests came up, interests that seemed to be genuine and even legitimate in themselves. You allowed the fire to burn low and the vision to fade out, and you never followed the Lord at all in the way He commanded. The Scripture does say in verse 31, they went forth. See the words towards the end of the verse: *they went forth with them from Ur of the Chaldees, to go into the land of Canaan.* The intention was to go all the way with God. However, the verse continues on to say, *and they came unto Haran, and dwelt there.* They were on their way to Canaan, but they came only so far as Haran, and they dwelt there out of the will of God. We should notice that *Terah* means *delay*, and that *Haran* means *dry ground.* How many a child of God, intending to go on to Canaan, to go all the way with God, has got only halfway? There has been delay; there has been a holding back. Now you are on dry ground instead of rejoicing in Canaan land. Now let us go on in the Genesis account to Genesis 12. It begins, *Now the LORD had said.* That small word *had* is intended to stir up your soul. Now God had already settled this matter; God had already made His will clear to Abraham. But Abraham is stuck, stuck at Haran, halfway to the land of Canaan; and God had said all the time, "Abraham, I want you in Canaan." **If you have come only halfway with God, you are not in the right place at all.** As long as Abraham went only halfway, he did not stand to receive the promise, and God Himself gave Abraham a definite promise.

Some information about Abraham not given until very much later.

Concerning that promise, Acts 7:2 records information not revealed in the Old Testament: ***The God of glory appeared unto our father Abraham, when he was in Mesopotamia, before he dwelt in Charran* [Haran]**, *And said unto him, Get thee out of thy country, and from thy kindred, and come into the land which I shall shew thee. Then came he out of the land of the Chaldeans, and dwelt in Charran* [Haran]: *and from thence, when his father was dead, he removed him into this land, wherein ye now dwell. And he gave him* *none inheritance in it, no, not so much as to set his foot on;* **yet he promised that he would give it to him for a possession, and to his seed after him, when as yet he had no child.** We learn here that God promised to give the land where He would lead Abraham, to him and to his seed; yet Abraham never received the land. He had only a small bit of territory that he finally bought for a grave. Acts 7:2-5 tells us that Abraham did not get even enough of the land for him to set foot on. Abraham journeyed for those one hundred years, walking around the land that God had promised him, surveying all the while the mountains and the valleys, the rivers and the seas. He looked at the land that God had promised, and he believed God; yet he never so much as set foot on it. I want to tell you that though Abraham has not yet received the land, he will. God will keep that promise. We know from Acts 7:2-5 that God will bless Abraham in keeping with every detail of the promise He originally gave. This passage informs us that the very God of glory appeared personally to Abraham when he was in Mesopotamia in far-off Ur of the Chaldees. This is a fact not recorded in the Old Testament, but it is given to us many years later in the book of Acts. Abraham actually met with God, and he believed God. And God counted it to him for righteousness. Christian friend, have you not yet come to see that God will keep His Word? You will not receive all that God has promised during your earthly journey, but God is not limited by time. What He promises, He will bring to pass someday. God is not slack concerning His promise. Wait on the Lord, and He shall bring it to pass. **When God gives the Word, He fulfills it.**

The seven-fold reward God had in store for Abraham.

As an encouragement to Abraham, God graciously gave him seven promises. Do you see them there in our key text? *Now the LORD had said unto Abram, Get thee out of thy country, and from thy kindred, and from thy father's house, unto a land that I will shew thee: And I will make of thee a great nation, and I will*

*bless thee, and make thy name great; and thou shalt be a blessing:
And I will bless them that bless thee, and curse him that curseth
thee: and in thee shall all families of the earth be blessed.* God gave
these promised blessings as marvellous incentives: "Abraham,
if you do this, here are seven blessings." Now you will never
truly give up one thing for the Lord, for you will find that the
Lord is no man's debtor. You cannot give up all in obeying
God and be a loser!

Let us look at these blessings. First, *I will make of thee a
great nation;* second, *I will bless thee;* third, *make thy name great;*
fourth, *thou shalt be a blessing.* **Oh, listen! Obey God now and
you will be a blessing.** If you fail the Lord now, the level of
blessing in your life has got to go down. In proportion as you
please God, as you obey God, you will be a blessing to others.
Fifth, *I will bless them that bless thee;* sixth, *and curse him that
curseth thee;* seventh, *and in thee shall all families of the earth be
blessed.*

As we look over these great blessings, we can see God
has placed emphasis on different people. In the first section,
you can see Abraham himself: *I will make of thee a great nation,
and I will bless thee, and make thy name great; and thou shalt be a
blessing.* Then in verse 3, there is reference to others: *I will bless
them that bless thee, curse him that curseth thee: and in thee shall
all families of the earth be blessed.* Thus, we see that in verse 2,
God speaks of Abraham, and in verse 3, He speaks of others.
This reminds us that no man lives unto himself. If you go
through with God, enter into covenant with God for His
blessing on your own soul, your life will be blessed and a
blessing to others. Look at verse 2 again. Here you see also an
application to Israel: *I will make of thee a great nation.* That nation
is Israel. If you look at verse 3, you can see the blessing reaching
out to all the earth, to all the families of the earth. That includes
you. You have shared in the blessing of Abraham, the blessing
of Christ, the blessing of the Gospel. You are part of all the
families of the earth. That is your household, your family.
Aye, you! As an individual, you are included here in the
promise.

The two things we need to know about every blessing
God gives.

We can learn two important lessons here. **First, blessing comes by bowing the knee.** What do I mean by that? It is a peculiar fact but a true one nevertheless that the word *blessing* in this portion of Scripture comes from a word that means to bend the knee. I find that most impressive. You cannot get the blessing of God, Abraham, unless you *bend the knee.* You cannot have the best that God has for you unless you bend the knee at the mercy seat. If you please God now, whatever it costs, you will discover that no man has ever lost by obeying God. Second, it is clear from this sevenfold blessing that **the blessing of God goes on for all eternity.** Sometimes when you go to a meeting, you may say, "You know, that was a great meeting. The singing was tremendous, I got a great lift, I felt the presence of God, I really got blessed there." What do we mean by that? Well, very often, we mean that on that night we were helped and encouraged, and our hearts were strangely warmed. But in the Bible, the blessing of God means a whole lot more than that. The blessing of God rolls on and on and on, for all eternity. All the families of the earth, not only in Abraham's day but on and on and on since that time, *continue* to receive God's blessing. We, too, have been sharing in the goodness of God. We have been blessed through the obedience of Abraham. We are blessed in Christ forever. Hallelujah!

> *The God of Abraham praise,*
> *Who reigns enthroned above;*
> *Ancient of everlasting days,*
> *And God of love.*
> *Jehovah, great I AM,*
> *By earth and heaven confessed;*
> *I bow and bless the sacred Name,*
> *Forever blest.*

The God of Abraham praise,
At Whose supreme command
From earth I rise, and seek the joys
At His right hand.
I all on earth forsake,
Its wisdom, fame, and power,
And Him my only portion make,
My shield and tower.

He by Himself hath sworn,
I on His oath depend,
I shall, on eagles' wings upborne,
To heaven ascend;
I shall behold His face,
I shall His power adore,
And sing the wonders of His grace
Forevermore.

The whole triumphant host
Give thanks to God on high;
"Hail, Father, Son, and Holy Ghost!"
They ever cry.
Hail, Abraham's God and mine!
I join the heavenly lays;
All might and majesty are Thine,
And endless praise.

CHAPTER THREE

INTO THE LAND -
ABRAHAM'S RESPONSE

" Now the Lord had said unto Abram, Get thee out of thy country, and from thy kindred, and from thy father's house, unto a land that I will shew thee: and I will make of thee a great nation, and I will bless thee, and make thy name great; and thou shalt be a blessing: And I will bless them that bless thee, and curse him that curseth thee: and in thee shall all families of the earth be blessed. So Abram departed, as the Lord had spoken unto him; and Lot went with him: And Abram was seventy and five years old when he departed out of Haran. And Abram took Sarai his wife, and Lot his brother's son, and all their substance that they had gathered, and the souls that they had gotten in Haran; and they went forth to go into the land of Canaan; and into the land of Canaan they came. "

Genesis 12:1-5

THE SCRIPTURE ADMONISHES US IN Isaiah 51:2, *Look unto Abraham your father, and unto Sarah that bare you: for I called him alone, and blessed him, and increased him.* When God says in this second verse of the chapter, "Look unto Abraham," He seems to be saying, "Go back to Genesis; study the life of Abraham and endeavour to follow in his steps. Look at him as an example and learn from his mistakes." Now the idea behind the word *look* in this place is to look, with a great deal of thought, intently if you like, with the heart, to Abraham your father. Remember God's promise to Abraham is still to be fulfilled. *You* also have yet to see all the promises of God fulfilled. Remember that Abraham received a call and began to follow that call. Do not be forgetful of *your* origins. Do not forget the starting point on the road to heaven. Every child of God will have occasion to look back to that hour when, by the call of God, he started out for Heaven and for home.

Obedience to God sometimes leads to a lonely path.

We now come back to the time that Abraham was sidetracked in Bypath Meadow. Remember that Abraham did not get all the way to Canaan the first time he set out. Perhaps we can see why Abraham fell into this trouble. Notice that little word *alone* in Isaiah 51:2, *for I called him alone.* According to our text, God had already spoken in the Ur of the Chaldees, making His will perfectly clear to Abraham with that threefold command: Abraham was to get out of his own country, he was to get away from his kindred, and he was to get away from his father's house. Yet, Genesis 12:5 informs us that Abraham *took Sarai his wife, and Lot his brother's son.* In addition, we know that Terah, Abraham's elderly father, was also in the company. We know that this situation was not what God had commanded, for the Lord had definitely indicated that discipleship would require that Abraham say goodbye to his father and goodbye to Lot whom he regarded as his own son. But things are not always as easy as they first appear.

I can imagine Terah, getting on in life, saying, "Don't leave me, Abraham. You are my son; I am putting all my dependence upon you. Remember I am your old father and I need you. After all, I am not getting any younger. I know God has called and I am sure there are blessings in store for you in Canaan land, but I am too old now to make it all the way there; however, I am prepared to leave the Ur of the Chaldees. I will forsake this land of idolatry and set out with you on the way to Canaan, but please don't leave me behind." Of course, we know they never managed to get there. Instead the family pitched their tents at Haran, and—if you consult the map of the Middle East—you can see that Haran, roughly speaking, is halfway to the land of Canaan. Now God speaks to us in all the details of the Bible. The history of the Bible is every bit as much inspired as the doctrine or the prophecy of Scripture; so when I look into historical events recorded inside the covers of the precious volume, I may see significant instruction for myself. Aye, and this detail of history reminds us that the child of God, instead of going all the way, may easily settle for less. Before we go on in this study, let me repeat that if you have come but halfway along the road to discipleship, halfway along the road to leaving all for Christ, then I pray God that the Lord will speak to you a little more.

Always there must be the kind of obedience which conforms exactly to the Word of God.

Happily, there is an afterwards for Abraham, and for us! We will now observe how the hand of God begins to work again in the life of this mighty man of faith. When his father was dead, Abraham came at last to the point of obedience. In Genesis 12:4, those touching words appear: *So Abram departed, as the Lord had spoken unto him.*

We must read on in this sentence and again we are reminded, *and Lot went with him.* Lot just went. Lot went with Abraham. Lot had no call from God to go to Canaan. He had no conviction as Abraham had to leave all for Jesus' sake. There was no heart in what Lot was doing. There is no record, for example, of Lot at prayer, or of Lot looking to the Lord for guidance before he made his way to Canaan. Oh, no. Lot was simply a fellow traveller. He could have gone to Canaan and, as the chapter shows, Lot could have gone just as cheerily to Egypt! Although Lot was a believer, a child of God, yet he seemed to be the kind of man who had no conviction. He had no strength of character. He seemed to be the kind of man who was one man one day, and a completely different man another day.

Oftentimes we find some professing the Lord's name who are like that. They don't show the kind of resolve that we would expect. We long to hear men and women say, "Lord, here is my heart. Let me, like Caleb of old, follow the Lord fully. Let there be no holding back, no vacillation." Oh, listen, nail your colours to the mast. If you mean to stand for the Lord, stand for Him now. Stand for Him without apology. Stand for Him with all your heart's affection. Don't be ashamed of the Lord but follow Him in earnest discipleship. Lot just went along. Listen, my Christian friend, *every step you take along the way of life must be in accordance with the Word of God.* Every association formed, every friendship forged must be in complete submission to the Scripture. We can see that this obedience is noted about Abraham in verse 4: *Abram departed, as the Lord had spoken unto him.* This obedience was not the case with Lot. God had not spoken to him about going to Canaan, and certainly God did not call him to take that step with Abraham. So we can learn from this passage that there are two classes of Christians: those who go by the Word—and they can look for the blessing of God—and those who, like Lot, merely go.

The costly business of disobedience weighed against the fulness of blessing God bestows on those who please Him.

Let me say to you that you can get out of the will of God. **You can miss out on God's best for your life.** The key to

Genesis chapter 12 lies right there at those words, *Get thee out.* Now God gave that command, as we all know, to Abraham when he was back there at the Ur of the Chaldees, and the strength of the passage here is, "Get thee out for thine own sake." Perhaps you should note that paraphrase in your Bible at this point, for we need to all remember that when God calls us to do something, He does not take special delight in a Christian's making some sort of sacrifice. Don't ever think that the Lord commands His people to do hard things without His providing a benefit for them somewhere else along the line. **The Lord is full of loving kindness; He always acts on behalf of His people.** When the Lord gives you direction, there is always a blessing just around the corner. You will never obey God for nothing. No man is a loser by following in the footsteps of the Saviour. Thank God we are not able to estimate the length and the depth and the breadth of God's fullness. Always there is more beyond for the believer. When the Lord says, "Abraham, get out of this place," the words are not spoken to him out of some expression of delight on God's part because He took Abraham away from his home place. Oh, no, the Lord has it in mind to make it worthwhile. It is for your own sake Abraham.

We must never allow people to imagine that if the Lord says to a Christian "Give that up," there is only a negative side to that direction. We are never to tell people, "Oh the Lord wants you to give this up or give that up," as if there is nothing else to the Christian life but giving up things. Nothing, I say nothing, can be further from the truth. It is true that there is an element of giving up in following the Lord. No man ever came to be a disciple of Christ—taking up his cross and following the Saviour—without having to forsake something. The disciples in the Gospel days left certain things, including their calling in life, as the Lord advised them to do; but on the positive side, they were given the very presence of the Lord Himself! They enjoyed the company of the Lord Jesus, walking in closest fellowship with Him, such as few have ever experienced. When God asks us to give up something in this life, He is about to bless us with something far better. The consolations of God are not small.

Abraham, then, would not leave Ur of the Chaldees as a deprived person. No, it was a privilege. Men and women, it is a privilege to meet with God. It is a privilege to receive God's Word and it is certainly a privilege as well as a joy to walk with the Lord. There is always more than before. God has blessings without number. The giving up of land and home was for Abraham's sake; and the call to follow the Lord, regardless of what you must give up, is also for *your* own good. Rather than spoiling your joy, the Lord will increase your joy. Rather than curtailing your freedom or your life, He will lead you on to greater fullness. It is for your own sake. Dear friend, is the Lord drawing you with the cords of love? Is He speaking to your soul about something that includes an element of sacrifice? Make no mistake about it; the Lord will more than make up for the apparent loss. I say "apparent loss" because you will find that you have lost nothing by following and honouring Him.

Take the world, but give me Jesus,
All its joys are but a name;
But His love abideth ever,
Thro' eternal years the same.

Take the world, but give me Jesus,
Sweetest comfort of my soul;
With my Saviour watching o'er me,
I can sing though billows roll.

Take the world, but give me Jesus,
Let me view His constant smile;
Then thro'out my pilgrim journey
Light will cheer me all the while.

Take the world, but give me Jesus,
In His cross my trust shall be;
Till, with clearer, brighter vision,
Face to face my Lord I see.

Oh, the height and depth of mercy!
Oh, the length and breadth of love!
Oh, the fullness of redemption,
Pledge of endless life above!

It is either the right place or the wrong place.

In our study of Abraham's pilgrimage, we will see him as an example of two distinct possibilities for every Christian: that of being in God's will and in God's place, and that of being out of God's will and in the wrong place altogether. Verses 4 to 9 of Genesis 12 show Abraham in the right place, that is in the land of Canaan, the Land of Promise. Then we find him in verses 10 to 20 in the land of Egypt, in the wrong place. You will recall how hard it was for Abraham to reach Canaan. His father's appeal and his family ties were demanding, perhaps even binding; consequently, Abraham fell short of obedience, for he took his father and nephew with him, rather than leaving them behind as God had instructed. What's more, he came to a stop on his way to Canaan and dwelt in Haran, rather than going the whole way. Eventually, Abraham did reach Canaan, but then we find that it was even more difficult to keep him there than it was to get him there. In the second instance, when Abraham was driven to go beyond the borders of Canaan, visiting the land of Egypt, he went too far. It seems that we as God's people are in a "strait betwixt two." Some fall short and would need to go on a little bit further along the way of following the Lord, and others have shot away beyond the boundary and have gotten themselves out of the will and place of God's direction.

The four characteristics of life in Canaan.

There are four characteristics of life in Canaan, that is of being in the will of God and enjoying obedience to him; and there are four characteristics of life in Egypt, that is of being out of God's will, of failing the Lord. It will fall to us, once we know these distinctions, to make our own judgments and somehow weigh ourselves in the balances of God. May we do so with the prayer that we would learn the disadvantages of straying from the Lord's commands, and experience the worthwhile benefits of living right in the centre of God's will. We are now at the place in following Abraham where we can learn some very, very powerful lessons. May we have special help from the sanctuary as we try to lay down these guidelines concerning the will of God.

First of all, **life in the land of Canaan is associated with pilgrimage.** It is God's will for the believer to engage in a pilgrimage. I will show you what that means. Look at the beginning of Genesis 12:6, *And Abram passed through.* Mark the words passed through, and read on a little further into the verse. *And Abram passed through the land unto the place of Sichem, unto the plain of Moreh. And the Canaanite was then in the land.* A word study here will reveal a vital truth to the believer. If you examine your Bible, the name Hebrew occurs in reference to the people of God only when it is used in speech by foreigners or to foreigners. Every instance where God's ancient people in Israel are called Hebrews, therefore, is when a distinction is made between them and other nations. The name Hebrew is special; its use is a means of separating God's people from the rest of men. **While you are here on this earth as a redeemed child of God, He wants you to be distinct from the rest of mankind.** Some of us are afraid of being different; we want a kind of anonymity that enables us to blend in with the rest of society. It is not God's will for you to walk that pathway. Since the Lord saved you and loved you and wrote down your name in the Lamb's Book of Life, He meant you to be an example and witness to the world. He did mean you to be different. The name *Hebrew* then is most significant.

Furthermore, the Hebrew is *one who does not belong here;* he is just passing through. It may surprise you if I say to you that these words *pass through,* derive from the very same root as that from which we get the word Hebrew. In a way, we could say of verse 6 that Abraham was acting the Hebrew, living out the part of the Hebrew while he *passed through the land* as one that did not belong. He was saying by his very manner of life, "I am a stranger here; I am just passing through." Notice how Genesis 14:13 describes Abraham: *And there came one that had escaped, and told Abram the Hebrew.* Do you see the testimony of the Holy Spirit about Abraham? This is the first time in the Bible when the name Hebrew is used as a classification, and Abraham is the first man to be honoured with that name. I will say this, he lived up to his name. Well did God give Abraham such a title, for by his example in everything, Abraham was the Hebrew. He belonged to the other side. He was just passing through. He was a stranger there.

Oh, do we need to say more? Is not God's Word like a mirror? When you stand in front of this mirror and gaze intently at what you see, instantly there is a revelation of your whole heart, soul and life. God wants you to know that you cannot, you dare not allow the roots of your life to get down too deeply into the world. There is that within every man and woman that strives to send down deep roots. It may be the new home you have. It may be the more permanent and satisfactory occupation that you have established, so that, as they say, you can "put your roots down." You can do no such thing. **The first characteristic of the child of God is that he is passing through this world.** He is not to be a permanent resident. The Lord tells you that Heaven is your home, and so it is. Meanwhile, you are not at home; you are merely passing through.

Further evidence of this truth appears in verse 8 in the word *removed*. The verse reads, *And he removed from thence unto a mountain on the east of Beth-el.* We can observe that the Canaanite was then in the land. All around Abraham were those who did not belong to God. Abraham was in the middle of them but, praise the Lord, he was passing through; he did not seek to abide with them. He did not make the mistake that Lot made. You would not find Abraham dwelling among them. In verse 9, Abraham journeyed, and once more he was a traveller. He was the Hebrew. He was passing through all the time. He was a man on a journey. Every Christian must know that he also is on a journey. Having left the City of Destruction he is making his way now to the Celestial City, the city of the Great King. So we have learned the meaning of the word *Hebrew,* and further, we have learned that Abraham himself is the Hebrew; and by his life and the prospect before him, he demonstrates very vividly for us all what it means to belong to the Lord *as one who is not at home in the world.* Hallelujah!

The second mark of the pilgrim is the presence of the Lord. Notice in verse 7 how twice over, the fact of the Lord's presence is made known: *And the Lord appeared unto Abram.* Again at the end of the verse, *the Holy Spirit records, and there builded he an altar unto the Lord, who appeared unto him.* Take note of the repetitions in the Bible. The Lord repeats those things that we need to take in. Rightly, God did not appear unto Abraham in Haran, the wrong place for Abraham to dwell. But now that Abraham has reached the land of Canaan and come into full obedience, the Lord has appeared unto him there. **God speaks to the believer when he is in the right place with Himself.** If it is your desire and prayer that the Lord would speak more and more to your soul, then seek for all that you are worth to be right in the centre of the will of God.

Third, a believer who walks in God's will seeks the Lord through the propitiatory work of Jesus Christ, or to put it simply, a yielded Christian worships on redemption ground. Again verse 7 tells us, *Unto thy seed will I give this land: and there builded he an altar unto the Lord.* This verse reminds us that all the blessings of God come to Abraham by way of the altar. Prayer and praise ascend to God from the altar, and the blessing of God descends upon the altar. Abraham worships the Lord on the ground of the redeeming blood. It is significant that Abraham in the right place with God is now building an altar. He worships there on redemption ground. Notice the blessing of God upon Abraham. Even the way God speaks to his soul and the way that the Lord makes His presence known to Abraham must not be passed over. We need to see that **God meets the Christian who worships on redemption ground.** We need to ask the Lord to teach us the power of the blood. In the spiritual place of prayer, in the place of conflict, in the place of following on to know the Lord, we will have to have recourse continually to the cross work of Christ. Abraham built an altar.

Many of us might be tempted to think that this point is obvious. We tend to say that of course we know about praying on redemption ground. We know that God hears our prayers when we stand before the throne of grace upon the merits of the propitiatory work of Jesus Christ. We know this basic theology. I admit that it seems to be a simple sort of a thing, but in practice the child of God is likely to forget this. Maybe I am talking about you. For example, you might be inclined to say sometime, "Well, as I pray, God will consider my prayer, seeing that I have separated myself from the world and from the apostasy." Perhaps you have thought, "God will hear my prayer seeing that I am a teacher now in the Sunday School and the Lord knows that I need the right lesson for the boys and the girls." Or perhaps you think, "God can see that it is my intention to follow Him and to live the Christian life to the best of my ability, and therefore He will recognize my prayer." Maybe in looking about at others you have reflected, "Since others have fallen away and I have kept going on with God, He will surely recognize the value of my prayers." Not a bit of it. You have made the very mistake we are talking about. You have shifted ground. Instead of building your prayer life on the shed blood of the Saviour, you have started now to build your prayer life on your own attainments. You have started to build your prayer life on your own reputation, on your own estimation of yourself. Listen, my friend, it is just as perilous for you to build your prayers upon *your* own works as it is for the ungodly man to build his prayers on *his* works. It is nothing but the blood of Jesus. If God accepts you, if He hears your prayers, if He receives your worship, if He speaks to you, it will not be because you are faithful, it will be because of Jesus' blood and righteousness.

Abraham's first thought is to build an altar. Genesis 12:7 tells us he builds an altar and worships the Lord. Abraham has learned to put the Lord first. By way of contrast, look at Genesis 11:4: *And they said, Go to, let us build us a city and a tower.* The first act of the ungodly peoples of the earth, who were gathered together at Babylon or Babel, was to build a city. Now the city is obviously different from the tent. The city holds quite a number of inhabitants. The city consists of maybe hundreds of houses, and these are permanent dwelling places. The city keeps its position. It does not move every five years, half a mile in this direction or five miles in that direction. Those who are in the city determine to send down their roots. This is the abiding place. The city is a fixture. But Abraham's first thought is to build an altar. To learn these hallmarks of the disciple's life in the land of Canaan, we must notice the importance of being a pilgrim—a man on a journey with no permanent abiding place; we also must notice the importance of the presence of the Lord; and we must see here that Abraham is praying at the altar—he cries to God on the strength of Christ's atoning work.

The last of the four characteristics of an obedient Christian life may be found in Genesis 12:8, *and* [he] *called upon the name of the Lord.* **The true believer's life is marked by prayer.** All the while Abraham is in the centre of the will of God, all the while he occupies territory in the land of Canaan, prayer characterizes his life. Abraham *called on the name of the Lord.* Prayer characterizes the life of a pilgrim, it is offered by one who is a stranger, it is breathed constantly by the one who stands only on the redeeming work of Christ. Are you on praying ground, my friend? Or have you moved away from God's will for your life? Until you draw near to Him in obedience, you will find that your prayers will be few and that the heavens will seem as brass. In the life of the obedient disciple, prayer is like breathing—necessary for life itself.

Let us keep these very important aspects of the Christian life in our minds— Pilgrimage, Presence of the Lord, Propitiation, Prayer—four very clear characteristics of Abraham's life when he is in the land of Canaan, the place of obedience.

The four characteristics of life in Egypt.

Come with me now to Egypt, for Abraham will journey onwards towards the south; and from the borders of the Land of Promise, he will make his way towards the kingdom of the Pharaohs. You will now see that there are also four other characteristics in Abraham's life as he moves into Egypt. I tremble as I think about them, because these same four marks—notice, I said the same four marks—appear in the life of any Christian when he gets away from God.

First, **life in Egypt is marked by declension.** I want you to notice the words in Genesis 12:10, *and Abram went down.* Do you see the simple statement? Abraham went *down*—he took a downward step. That is always the direction of the first step in separation from God. Abraham went down to Egypt. The Scripture always portrays Egypt as a type of the world. Consequently, as Abraham leaves the Land of Promise where God wants him to be, and makes his journey towards Egypt, he is not going up. It is not an upward way; it is a downward path. God knows all of our hearts. Have some of us become uneasy in the direction this study has taken us? Remember, we are looking into the mirror of God that gives us a true picture. What does it tell us? **Once you are out of the will of God, once your steps lead you towards the world, you are declining.** You will slip ever downward. We have seen it in young people, so fascinated by the world. We have also seen it in those who are very much older and ought to know better.

We have seen it in mature Christians. We have seen it in men saved for years, who have sat in the prayer meetings, who have read and studied their Bibles. We have seen it in men who in former times were exceedingly used and blessed of God in His work, but who in recent times have been going downhill. God takes note of it. Oh, this is exceedingly sobering, and it pains me to talk about Abraham on the way down. I can scarcely take it in that Abraham, such a valiant servant of God, should take a downward step.

Men and women, the Genesis record of this part of Abraham's life should solemnize our hearts, for it shows us that even in the best of men, even in the best of God's people, there can be a going down in the Christian life. I have to say therefore, that if these past days, months, or years have found you in a downward path, I beg you in God's name to stop dead in your tracks. Know for sure that the mind of God is being given to you. You are in a dreadfully dangerous position, for you are out of the will and the blessing of God.

Some very special teaching about Egypt from the book of Jeremiah.

Jeremiah 42:13-16 can give us insight into the attraction which Egypt has for the pilgrims of God, as well as its dangers. *But if ye say, We will not dwell in this land, neither obey the voice of the LORD your God, saying, No; but we will go into the land of Egypt, where we shall see no war, nor hear the sound of the trumpet, nor have hunger of bread; and there will we dwell: and now therefore hear the word of the LORD, ye remnant of Judah: Thus saith the LORD of hosts, the God of Israel: If ye wholly set your faces to enter into Egypt, and go to sojourn there; Then it shall come to pass, that the sword, which ye feared, shall overtake you there in the land of Egypt, and the famine, whereof ye were afraid, shall follow close after you there in Egypt; and there ye shall die.* The group of people in this passage who are saying, "No," belong to the people of Israel, God's own people. They are at a crossroads. They have to decide whether to stay in the land of Israel—which is the command of the Lord to them—or whether to go down to Egypt. These people are facing hardship and danger in the land where the Lord has called them. They perceive Egypt to be a better, an easier dwelling place for the time. This dilemma is a bit like the decision Abraham had to make. There was a famine in the land of Canaan; there was trouble ahead, and Abraham considered what he should do.

The temptation in Bible times, the temptation for people in the land of Israel, was always to go to Egypt. The temptation for *you*, my Christian friend, all the while you are here in this earthly life, is for you to turn to the world. It doesn't take much to get God's people into the world. We have all seen it happen. Perhaps some Christian gets offended, and before you know what has happened, he is away from the Lord and into the world. It is easy for a believer to make a mistake or to become forgetful and careless or perhaps to be overwhelmed and discouraged, and be drawn away and enticed of his own lusts, and slide right down into the ways of the world. Perhaps a young person has got himself in with a certain crowd. On Friday night the arrangement is made. These companions are planning to get into the car to go some miles down the road to a destination or activity that this young person knows is not God's will. He can't refuse for fear of ridicule. He wants to be part of the crowd. These people, like Abraham in the land of Israel, are tempted to go to Egypt. But God is saying, "No, don't go there."

The people in Jeremiah 42 were not wise, for they actually said no to God! When men say no, when they disobey, we can have only one word for them. We have to say: "Look, when you choose to turn your back on God's will and turn to the world, when you are saying no, you are not just saying no to the church, you are not just saying no to the minister, you are not just saying no to your parents; you are saying no to the Lord. You would need to learn to say no to Egypt. You would need to learn to say no to the world. You have been saying no to the Lord far too long." What does God say to those who contemplate breaking His commands? Listen to His words in

Deuteronomy 10:12, 13, *And now, Israel, what doth the LORD thy God require of thee, but to fear the LORD thy God, to walk in all his ways, and to love him, and to serve the LORD thy God with all thy heart and with all thy soul, To keep the commandments of the LORD and his statutes, which I command thee this day for thy good?*

The beautiful face of the temptress of Egypt.

But what was so tempting about Egypt at the time described in Jeremiah 42? The attraction was that Egypt was at peace. She was quiet from war. It seems that there is always war in Israel; there is always trouble wherever the people of God are. And to people who battle constantly, it seems as if there is nothing to bother the soul in Egypt—nothing there but tranquility. It is the world's idea of Heaven. It appears that there is no scarcity in the world. We will not want for bread and we will never hear the sound of the trumpet. We will never be asked to do anything hard. We will not be under orders. What a lie! Oh, what a fool that man is who is taken in by the world and dragged into the snare of the devil. You think that in the world you can do what you like and you can go where you like, but you cannot. The world is the devil's playground, and he makes the rules. Listen, you cannot go where you like and you cannot do what you like and obey God at the same time. Oh, it is far better to dwell in the land of God's choosing and endure battle, than to separate yourself from His safety, protection and blessing in order to be at ease. It is far better, Abraham, to have a famine in the land of Israel and be there with God, than to be down in Egypt where you will have the promise of prosperity, but at the same time, the problem of being out of the will of God. What a powerful realization that is.

> *I must have the Saviour with me,*
> *For I dare not walk alone;*
> *I must feel His presence near me,*
> *And His arm around me thrown.*

I must have the Saviour with me,
For my faith, at best is weak;
He can whisper words of comfort
That no other voice can speak.

I must have the Saviour with me,
In the onward march of life,
Thro' the tempest and the sunshine,
Thro' the battle and the strife. —

I must have the Saviour with me,
And His eye the way must guide,
Till I reach the vale of Jordan,
Till I cross the rolling tide.

Then my soul shall fear no ill,
Let Him lead me where He will;
I will go without a murmur,
And His footsteps follow still.

Furthermore, the Egypt life is characterized by dishonesty. Read verse 10 and following of Genesis, chapter 12. *And there was a famine in the land; and Abram went down into Egypt to sojourn there; for the famine was grievous in the land. And it came to pass, when he was **come near** to enter into Egypt, that he said unto Sarai his wife. . .say, I pray thee, thou art my sister.* As we continue in this account, we notice that the nearer Abraham got to Egypt, the more like Egypt he became. Egypt was full of people who did not know the living God. Their ways were not God's ways. Abraham, on the other hand, was the follower of the one true God; yet we find as he drew near to Egypt, that he began to deal with his circumstances as those in Egypt might have done. *When he was **come near** to enter into Egypt. . . he said unto Sarai his wife. . .say. . .thou art my sister.* Abraham began to fear. He decided to lie. We find, as events unfolded, that Abraham not only told the lie, but he started to live the lie. Sarah was taken to live in another man's house. How far

down can a Christian go? Oh Abraham, you prayed; you intended to follow the Lord fully. Abraham, you built that altar and you pitched your tent at
Beth-el, and you meant it. But now you have gone down. You have gone down so far that you have imagined that it would be right to tell the lie.
Let me stop here and give a word to someone in need. God knows your heart. Have you gone down so far that you are living a lie? Are you living by double standards, professing one thing but living another kind of life altogether? Child of God, if that be your situation, you are quickly going downhill. You can lose your testimony. You can tell the lie and lose out with God. What does this passage tell us about ourselves? Egypt, in Scripture, is the type of the world. The conclusion is not difficult: the *closer* to the world we come, the more *like* it we become. This world is not a safe place for the Christian. We cannot dwell in the world and remain free of its filth and deception.

In addition, **we find is that the child of God in Egypt eventually encounters disaster.** In verse 16 of this chapter we find the words, *And he* [Pharaoh] *entreated Abram well for her sake.* Abraham had sheep and oxen, asses, men servants, maidservants, she asses and camels. Oh, it seemed as though the man called Abraham was getting on wonderfully well in the land of Egypt. His plan was working beautifully. How the devil can fool the believer. He gives you a few toys to play with and you imagine that all is well. Abraham, I say, is prospering. He is doing well in the land of Egypt, but all the while in his own soul he has lost out with the Lord. He has gone down. Verse 17 explodes the dream: *And the Lord plagued Pharaoh and his house with great plagues, because of* — because of the sin of Pharaoh? No. Because of the idolatry of Egypt? No. Because of the wickedness of the heathen in that vast empire? No. *Because of Sarai Abram's wife.* Because of Abraham's lie. Because of dishonesty. Because of the way Abraham has lost out with the Lord. Now what do we see in Abraham? He who should have been a blessing — *in thee shall all families of the earth be blessed* — becomes a *curse* to the people of the land. His life is a disaster. But God had promised in verse 3 that He would make Abraham a blessing. How then, by the time we get to verse 17, do we find that he is a plague and a curse? He is the very opposite of a blessing. He is a disaster to everyone around him. Has the Lord forgotten His promise? Has the Lord gone back on His word? On the contrary, God is being true to His Word. **The Lord undertakes to do great things for His people while they are in the centre of His will.** Remember what we noted at the very beginning of this study: God's people will be blessed and a blessing when they bend the knee, when they humbly bow at the feet of their Lord and King. Let the child of God wander away, let him go downhill, let him turn his back on God's will and God's place, let him make for Egypt, and as he gets near to Egypt, he begins to take on the lifestyle of the heathen. Instead of being a blessing he becomes a plague and a curse. Abraham is only a blessing when he is in **the land.**

Do you see what it means to lose your testimony? You become a blight; you become a stumbling block. There is Pharaoh, an ungodly man, and his household is actually plagued because of the man of God who has come into his land, a man of God, who for the time being, has forgotten the will of the Lord for his life. You have to think very carefully about your testimony and how you live. The Lord saves you to be a channel for good and not for evil. Romans 2:24 states that the nation of Israel fell into the same sin: *For the name of God is blasphemed among the Gentiles through you* [Israel]. God says in this book that He intended the whole nation to be a channel for good among the nations of the earth; but instead of being a channel for good, Israel turned her back on God, becoming a plague and curse throughout the nations of the earth, and a cause for blasphemy. Do you see this, disobedient Christian? You have caused the enemies of the Lord to blaspheme. That word *blaspheme* includes criticism, false accusation, slander and cursing. God is saying that by your sin, you can actually cause the name of the Lord to be blasphemed.

Last, we have to see that **the life in Egypt will always bring great disappointment.** By disappointment, I mean becoming disillusioned with the world, disappointed in Egypt, out of which Abraham had come to expect so much. In verse 19, we have Pharaoh reproaching Abraham, saying, *Why saidst thou, She is my sister? So I might have taken her to me to wife: now therefore behold thy wife, take her, and go thy way.* The word go in this passage is very strong. It means that Pharaoh is saying literally, "Take her and go, get out of here!" Sometimes the wayward Christian will find things turning out very awkwardly for him, and he might even wonder why, chastened in heart and in soul, these things have worked out so badly. Abraham intended to go down to Egypt so that he could do better there than he was doing in the impoverished land of Canaan. He wanted the good Egypt offered, and he did, by his plan, increase in sheep, oxen, asses, men servants, maidservants, she asses and camels. He might have written a letter home saying, "God is blessing me powerfully here." But the truth of the matter was that he was just a plague and not a blessing. How disappointing! How disillusioning that Pharaoh should say, "Here is your wife; now you pack your bags and get out of here." There are times when things go horribly wrong for the Christian because he has not prayed. There are times when things go horribly wrong for the believer and God has called that one to Himself because things are just not right.

Take her and go. Do you see that Pharaoh is offended? He is offended in finding out Abraham's lies. There is no such thing as telling one lie. It is not possible to tell only one lie. You will need to tell another to back it up, and you will have to tell another one to back up those two. So once you have started on the wrong track, you are in real trouble. It is necessary for the Christian, even if it is unpleasant, just to face up to the truth. Pharaoh throws Abraham's lies right in his teeth. The ungodly man with whom he had come to work reproaches him and puts him in his place. What an embarrassment, what a disillusioning experience, what a disappointment! Instead of Abraham's playing the prince he certainly was (for he was the child of God), instead of Abraham's demonstrating the blessing of God to a heathen king (for he was the man to whom the promise of the blessing had come), instead of Abraham's instructing Pharaoh (for Abraham talked with God), Abraham was rebuked, rejected, and run out of town. Egypt robbed Abraham of all the benefits that he had so richly experienced while he had walked with the Lord in the land of Canaan.

Out of the will of God. You can follow in detail Abraham's downward steps to Egypt—no altar, no record of prayer, no appearing of the Lord. Those vital marks of life, the life of the pilgrim, the life of the Hebrew in the land of Canaan are beginning to disappear. Now Abraham's life is marked by Declension, Dishonesty, Disaster, and Disappointment. Oh Abraham, what have you lost now that you have taken those steps? Dear believer, I pray that you will search your soul. As you have watched Abraham, has your heart been melted? What have you lost in your downward pathway into the world? You have lost out in prayer. You have lost out in the building of the altar. You have lost out on those precious times with God for which nothing else in the world will ever compensate. What should you do? Hear the voice of the Father. His voice calls you home.

> *God is calling the prodigal, come without delay,*
> *Hear, O hear Him calling, calling now for thee;*
> *Tho' you've wandered so far from His presence, come today,*
> *Hear His loving voice calling still.*

The Christian who truly wants restoration will seek to return to the presence of his heavenly Father. His heart will echo the hymn writer who penned these very familiar words:

I've tired of sin and straying, Lord,
Now I'm coming home;
I'll trust Thy love, believe Thy word,
Lord, I'm coming home.

"Yes," you say, "that is my heart's cry. I want to get back to the place of blessing. I want to be once again in God's will, basking in His smile, hearing His voice. But *how* can I go back? I've strayed so far; I've been so foolish. What is the way back?"

My friend, if you truly repent and desire to leave the world behind, look once more into that blessed mirror of God. Abraham found the way back. Genesis 13:1-4 tells us, *And Abram went up out of Egypt, he and his wife, and all that he had, and Lot with him, into the south. And Abram was very rich in cattle, in silver, and in gold. And he went on his journeys from the south even to Beth-el unto the place where his tent had been at the beginning, between Beth-el and Hai; Unto the place of the altar, which he had made there at the first: and there Abram called on the name of the LORD.* How the Holy Spirit heaps words upon words that we might not miss His message! Abraham knew he had to go back to the place where he started, back to Beth-el, back to the place of the altar. Watch it carefully, *he went. . .even to Beth-el. . .where his tent had been at the beginning . . .Unto the place of the altar, which he had made there at the first.* And what was the first blessing that God restored to Abraham? Prayer, fellowship with God Himself!. . .*and there Abram called on the name of the LORD.* What is the significance of the altar? It is the picture of God's great sacrifice for sin, the precious shed blood. It is the place of the Cross of Jesus Christ, Who died to take away our sins. Where did you begin in your Christian walk? What was your first experience of God's love and pardon? It began at the foot of the Cross. You knelt there in repentance and found God's love, cleansing, and pardon. That's where it all began, and that is the way back. Go back with Abraham to the altar. You will find your way home.

I must needs go home by the way of the cross,
There's no other way but this;
I shall ne'er get sight of the gates of light,
If the way of the cross I miss.

I must needs go on in the blood-sprinkled way,
The path that the Saviour trod,
If I ever climb to the heights sublime,
Where the soul is at home with God.

Then I bid farewell to the way of the world
To walk in it nevermore;
For my Lord says, "Come," and I seek my home
Where He waits at the open door.

The way of the cross leads home,
The way of the cross leads home;
It is sweet to know, as I onward go,
The way of the cross leads home.

And so we end this chapter in a very happy place. Abraham is back where he belongs—in the Land of Promise, once more in the will of God, in the place of the altar. May this experience be ours as well. Hallelujah for the Cross!

CHAPTER FOUR

BETWEEN ME AND THEE - ABRAHAM'S CONFLICT

❝ *And Abram was very rich in cattle, in silver, and in gold . . . And Lot also, which went with Abram, had flocks, and herds, and tents. And the land was not able to bear them, that they might dwell together: for their substance was great, so that they could not dwell together. And there was a strife between the herdmen of Abram's cattle and the herdmen of Lot's cattle: and the Canaanite and the Perizzite dwelled then in the land. And Abram said unto Lot, Let there be no strife, I pray thee, between me and thee, and between my herdmen and thy herdmen; for we be brethren. Is not the whole land before thee? separate thyself, I pray thee, from me: if thou wilt take the left hand, then I will go to the right; or if thou depart to the right hand, then I will go to the left. And Lot lifted up his eyes, and beheld all the plain of Jordan, that it was well watered every where, before the LORD destroyed Sodom and Gomorrah, even as the* *garden of the LORD, like the land of Egypt, as thou comest unto Zoar. Then Lot chose him all the plain of Jordan; and Lot journeyed east: and they separated themselves the one from the other.* **/ /**

Genesis 13:2, 5-11

TIMES OF CONFLICT AND TESTING often follow hard on the heels of spiritual victory. Such was the experience of the man of God in this passage. Abraham had finally returned to the land of blessing, to Beth-el, the place of the altar. There he *called on the name of the LORD.* The peace in his own soul, which surely had come when he returned to Canaan and met with God, must have been a blessed relief after the experiences of Egypt. Yet, things were not to remain peaceful.

In God's work, even in times of revival, people show their weaknesses. Even in the best of times, God's people are still in the flesh and sometimes act so. Notice the phrase in verse 5: *And Lot also, which went with Abram.* Lot here is associated with Abraham, identified with him. This phrase is like saying, "So-and-so went to your church, didn't he? I think I remember his attending." This is exactly the same type of expression. Lot, being closely involved with Abraham, reflected upon that godly man simply by association, and as this story unfolds, we shall see that Abraham suffered from Lot's foolish actions. Here we have a ready-made situation. It is as if someone said, "You know that church member who attends down the street? Well, do you know what he did?" If tongues are going to wag, if people are going to point the finger, here we have the start of such a situation. This is the man who went with Abraham.

Scripture goes on to tell us, *And the land was not able to bear them, that they might dwell together:* for their substance was great, so that they could not dwell together. Sometimes material blessings are not blessings at all. Mind you, I can understand anyone praying for a blessing, even in material things. We have need for food, shelter, and clothing just as other people, and we may well ask the Lord for our needs, and even for our wants. But sometimes when we pray for a blessing we may not know for what we are praying. Perhaps we pray, "Oh, give me that. Would you do that for me? Please, Lord, do it for me." We do not always ask wisely. We do not always think carefully about what we ask. And we do not always carefully seek the will and the glory of the Lord in the matter.

But let us suppose we have received a blessing from the Lord that has prospered us and helped us on our way in life. How have we responded? Sometimes when the Lord does good things for us or bestows His love on us in a tangible way, we act shamefully. We fail Him. Is not verse 6 terribly sad? *The land was not able to bear them that they might dwell together, for. . .*What was the reason that they could not live together in peace? They were so poor? No, *for their substance was great.* If they had been so poor that they had hardly a dozen in the flock, perhaps things would have gone much better. No, when God is good to us materially and helps us through those difficult times, it is not always the best for the soul. The body may do well, but the soul may dry up and shrivel. It is a sad thing for Christians to be at war with one another. It is a sad thing for God's people to fall out. It is even worse if they fall out over money.

The sad discovery of strife among the people of God.

Verse 7 tells us that there was *strife between the herdmen of Abram's cattle and the herdmen of Lot's cattle.* This is quarrelling between two households of relatives! It is a shameful thing to see division among brethren. **It certainly is not God's will that there should be disharmony in the church.** Every Christian who is active in a fellowship of believers should pray for the unity of that church. You need to pray against the subtlety of the devil. The work of the Lord within a congregation can be hindered greatly if there are divisions and strife among God's people, and these problems creep in very easily unless each member is actively praying for the unity of the Spirit in the church.

Sometimes the most trivial matter brings division in the camp of God. Years ago, I heard of a difficulty in a church. There was a family in the congregation that had rendered sterling service for years. Someone thought the church should honour this family by presenting a clock in their name to be hung in the house of God. The night of the presentation was a joyful time, and the clock was hung above the doors of the entrance. Soon, someone came through those doors and commented, "This is no place for the clock. It is the worst place in the whole church to have the clock. Why don't you put the clock on this wall?" So, with some embarrassment and probably with offence to the person who had decided it should go above the doors, the clock was put on the other wall. Once more, this was a matter of offence, and after a "to-ing and fro-ing" in the congregation, the clock had to be moved yet another time. Finally, we heard that several members were ready to leave the church over it. What a triviality! It would have been better to throw the clock out through the window if it would be the means of keeping peace in the house of God. We may laugh over such a ridiculous situation; but in the end, the Lord is grieved, God's people are out of fellowship with Him and each other, and bitterness and evil have come in. Aye, and over nothing, over absolutely nothing!

There is no issue that I know of—and I want to state this carefully—there is no issue that I know of important enough to have the work of God wrecked. The devil holds high carnival when he can turn the artillery of God's people upon the rest of the people of God. It is not God's will for you to be at variance with another Christian. If in some way, a difference has crept in and destroyed the fellowship and your joy in coming to the house of God, the time has come for you to get on your knees and have the whole thing in its entirety prayed out of your soul. You grieve the Lord when you indulge in whims like these.

The vexation of Christians committing sin before the ungodly.

This time of strife was an unhappy time in Abraham's life, and certainly it was an even worse time for Lot who bore his own guilt in the matter. Still, we have not seen the worst of the situation. Verse 7 reminds us, *the Canaanite and the Perizzite dwelled then in the land.* What is the meaning of the word *then?* The word means, *at the same time.* This trouble between the brethren took place in the presence of the enemy. Very simply, these men quarrelled in front of the ungodly. The Lord is saying that just then, when strife was raging in the camp where prayer ought to have been heard, just then the Canaanite and Perizzite were on every side. It was not a good witness for those who belonged to the camp that the difficulty between them could not be solved. Oh, you must consider not only your relationship with other believers, and your relationship with the Lord Himself, but surely you will want to keep in mind the ungodly. When there is trouble in the camp of God the people in the neighbourhood soon get to hear of it. It is a crying shame that sometimes Christians have been unwise, and because of their own selfish thoughts, they have been prepared to put the whole work of God and the testimony of Christ at risk. There is nothing so important as to cause you to wreck the work of God for it. The ungodly are watching you. You have to live the life. It is good to pray. It is right to persevere in the things of God. Of course, you should be zealous and fly the flag high for the Saviour, but remember this: there must be practical Christianity. The Lord wants you to live the life. Pray that you will never let the Lord down. Pray that you will never drag the name of the Lord into the gutter. Pray, "Lord, help me to do right." Remember, practical Christianity is required of you by the Lord. It is not enough to know all the right things and be courageous in giving forth the Gospel. You must live the life too, so that in matters of right and wrong, your hands are clean. **In matters of conscience, your life needs to be pure**.

Abraham and Lot - very rich - are "weighed down" with the
care of worldly things.

This strife among brethren, conducted in the presence of
the enemy, arose from interest in worldly things. Notice verse
2 and also verses 5 and 6. Abraham is now very rich, (literally,
"heavy" or "weighed down") in cattle, silver, and gold. Now
he had cattle, silver, and gold before he went to Egypt, but it
is clear from the careful reading of chapter 12 that Abraham
prospered in material things while he lived in Egypt. Lot also
did very well when he was in Egypt for he had his own
personal flocks, herds and tents. When verse 6 says *the land
was not able to bear them, that they might dwell together*, the
proximity of the words *dwell together*, emphasizes the fact that
there was no "togetherness" or unity between Abraham and
Lot. All this was because of their interest in material things.
The sequel to this upheaval, however, seems to indicate that
Abraham kept right values all the time, and remained in
fellowship with God, while Lot did not do so; therefore, I take
the view that Lot was to blame all the while for the unrest. Lot
got interested in worldly things. He could not dwell with
Abraham.

The fact was that Lot could not dwell with Abraham in
the tents of prayer, but he certainly could dwell in the cities of
the plain. I have known people to leave the church over some
particular issue, and before long, they are found in some other
gathering of Christian people, not only tolerating the thing
that they could not tolerate before, but tolerating a hundred
other things that are far worse. Indeed, we shall find that Lot
tolerated so much sin and filth in Sodom, that his soul was
vexed day by day. Oh, when the heart is not right, when a
Christian is out of sorts with God, it is just incredible the kinds
of things he might do.

The magnanimity of a mighty man of God.

So how did Abraham conduct himself in the midst of this

conflict? I believe that Abraham demonstrated a life which took care to keep a pure conscience before God and man. He was a noble man, generous in spirit, large of heart. Bear in mind, that Lot never had any word from God to go to the land of Canaan, and he had no business being there. He never had any promise from God as to an inheritance. Abraham could have said to Lot, "Just you get as far away from me as you can. Clear off of this territory. God has said this is my land, and although I do not possess it yet, this land is for me. You need to pray to God for yourself, and get a share of territory from the Lord that you can call your own, but don't stay here in my domain." Nothing like these words ever came from Abraham's lips. Instead, we see Abraham's generosity of spirit in verse 8: *Let there be no strife, I pray thee, between me and thee, and between my herdmen and thy herdmen.* Although the herdsmen went to war, Abraham brought himself into the conflict. He took responsibility for the situation. He said, "There ought not to be strife between the two of us, never mind the herdsmen. Let us resolve this problem in a peaceful manner." This situation could be compared to two employers today who attend the same church. Perhaps your employees run into a disagreement with the people who work for the other person. Then your workers report this problem to you at the office. You could react to this negative report. You could allow a kind of hardness to enter into your own soul. You could then develop a problem with the person who attends your church. No, Abraham is doing the righteous thing here. Instead of insisting upon his own rights, he makes peace. He says, "Don't let us fall out over this thing. Don't let the devil get in. Don't let this thing get through to us." *Let there be no strife, I pray thee, between me and thee.*

When strife erupts, there is a fault or cause somewhere. Someone has done wrong. In this context, pray to God that the thing will not get into *your* soul. "Lord, please don't let this conflict come to me, and if it comes, do not allow it to come between me and this other brother." More importantly, you need to pray that such a situation will not tempt you to break fellowship with the Lord. That is the very worst conceivable result. If bitterness of soul, if hardness of heart have crept in between you and the Lord, if that old poison has got into your heart, you know about it. If this has happened to you, it is choking off your spiritual life. The sooner you are rid of it, the better, *for we be brethren.* Don't you forget that.

God's people do not always see eye to eye. It is no use pretending that we will. Even within a single small congregation, there is never complete agreement. It is a human impossibility. Aye, there is awkwardness in God's work sometimes, but the child of God who starts working in the flesh is never going to please the Lord or do God's work effectively. You cannot do God's work with resentment toward the brethren. For we be brethren. Remember this. Even though the difference is there, try to pray it out of your soul. You will have a difference sometimes along the way with one or more of God's saints, but remember during that time this does not mean these people are not the Lord's. This does not mean that you are snow-white clean. This does not mean that you can go your way and content yourself that you have been right all along, and that they have been one hundred per cent in the wrong. Life is not like that. It takes two to pick a fight. Even though there are two sides to every conflict, and very likely one side is more to blame than the other, there still will arise faults on both sides. To the utmost of your power, ask the Lord to tear away any root of bitterness in your heart. Go into your room and shut the door. Stay there on your knees with your Bible until you have got the thing cleared out. And remember, only the Lord Himself can rid you of such sin.

Going the second mile for God.

We have talked about Abraham's generosity of spirit. We pointed out that this man of God kept his conscience clear, and strove to maintain peace in a potentially explosive situation. But Abraham's generous spirit went the extra mile. Though he owed Lot nothing, though he alone possessed the promise of land, Abraham gave up his right to sole possession. He even went so far as to offer Lot first choice of the territory. *Is not the whole land before thee? Separate thyself, I pray thee, from me: if thou wilt take the left hand, then I will go to the right; or if thou depart to the right hand, then I will go to the left.* The point of separation had been reached. Sometimes in God's work, separation must occur, although we don't like it. If it must happen, let us try to be like Abraham and say, "There is the whole land; we are brethren."

Genesis 13:10-13 tells us, *And Lot lifted up his eyes, and beheld all the plain of Jordan, that it was well watered every where, before the LORD destroyed Sodom and Gomorrah, even as the garden of the LORD,, like the land of Egypt, as thou comest unto Zoar. Then Lot chose him all the plain of Jordan; and Lot journeyed east: and they separated themselves the one from the other. Abram dwelled in the land of Canaan, and Lot dwelled in the cities of the plain, and pitched his tent toward Sodom. But the men of Sodom were wicked and sinners before the LORD exceedingly.* Watch carefully a separation between God's people. If one party has not put things right, then from the point of separation onwards, that man goes down, sometimes very, very quickly. Even if there must be a separation, it is a special time to remain guarded and extremely cautious. If there be no way to work together, if both parties have chastened their own hearts, both sides prayed, then perhaps the Lord will overrule all things for His own name's sake and bless in an equal fashion on both sides. But I must say that if there is not real heart-searching prayer and repentance, the man who is in the wrong can go from blessing to chastening, and from there to shame and sorrow, in some cases, never to walk in the full blessing of the Lord again in this life. And what a grievous position for a Christian.

So, in the conflict, Abraham gave up his rights for conscience' sake, indeed, for the Lord's sake. He separated from Lot on the best terms possible. Lot seemed to get the choice land, but we shall see in the ensuing chapter that Lot's life ended in tragedy. Abraham, on the other hand, was blessed immeasurably by God. He understood that true blessings were not temporal. Further, God called Himself *the friend of Abraham!* What peace of heart, what blissful fellowship Abraham enjoyed with his Friend. In the conflict, Abraham experienced victory. His response to this difficulty reminds us of the instruction in Micah 6:8, *He hath shewed thee, O man, what is good; and what doth the LORD require of thee, but to do justly, and to love mercy, and to walk humbly with thy God?* Oh that we might follow the Lord wholly, dealing with every conflict in the light of God's love and patience toward us, and in a way that would bring glory to His name and blessing to His people.

> *Search me, O God, and know my heart today;*
> *Try me, O Saviour, know my thoughts I pray.*
> *See if there be some wicked way in me;*
> *Cleanse me from ev'ry sin and set me free.*
>
> *I praise Thee, Lord, for cleansing me from sin;*
> *Fulfill Thy Word and make me pure within.*
> *Fill me with fire where once I burned with shame,*
> *Grant my desire to magnify Thy name.*
>
> *Lord, take my life and make it wholly Thine;*
> *Fill my poor heart with Thy great love divine.*
> *Take all my will, my passion, self and pride;*
> *I now surrender, Lord—in me abide.*
>
> *O Holy Ghost, revival comes from Thee;*
> *Send a revival—start the work in me.*
> *Thy Word declares Thou wilt supply our need;*
> *For blessings now, O Lord, I humbly plead.*

CHAPTER FIVE

IN THE GATE OF SODOM - ABRAHAM'S NEPHEW

" Abram dwelled in the land of Canaan, and Lot dwelled in the cities of the plain, and pitched his tent toward Sodom. But the men of Sodom were wicked and sinners before the LORD exceedingly. "

Genesis 13:12.13

" . . . and Lot sat in the gate of Sodom . . . "

Genesis 19:1

// And delivered just Lot, vexed with the filthy conversation of the wicked: (For that righteous man dwelling among them, in seeing and hearing, vexed his righteous soul from day to day with their unlawful deeds;) The Lord knoweth how to deliver the godly out of temptations, and to reserve the unjust unto the day of judgment to be punished: //

II Peter 2:7-9

LOT HAD GONE DOWN TO dwell in Sodom. Of course, he ought to have known better; he should never have been there in the first place. *The men of Sodom were wicked and sinners before the LORD exceedingly.* You would think that Lot would be doing the worst kind of evil in choosing a place to live where its inhabitants were called wicked. That was bad enough. But the Scripture further emphasizes that that the men of Sodom were *sinners before the LORD exceedingly.* This description is even worse. The words *before the LORD* means that the men of Sodom could sin with a brazen, hard-hearted, defiant attitude. They could sin in the very face of God. They could sin with impunity. It seems that these men did not have one thought of repentance. They could perform their sinful actions as if they were aware and yet unafraid, though all the while God was looking down from Heaven upon them. They would say with a hard spirit, without conscience, without regret or desire to change, "Well, this is the way we are living—and so what?" They were exceedingly wicked sinners before God. These were the people among whom Lot chose to dwell!

How we know Lot is saved - the testimony of scripture.

Some might be tempted to question Lot's salvation. Indeed, if we were to limit our reading to only the Old Testament account of Lot's life, we would learn about the man sitting in the gate of Sodom. We would see this man do wrong, and learn that he allowed strife to enter into his soul. We would find that he disregarded God's will. But we would not know about his standing before God. We have, however, additional information about Lot given to us in the New Testament. II Peter 2:7 says, *And delivered just Lot.* What does the word *just* mean? It means *justified.* Our Bible teaches us that the justified man is a saved man. The Holy Ghost is saying that although our judgment might well have been different concerning Lot's standing before God, this wayward man, this nephew of Abraham, was justified by God, and therefore saved and on his way to Heaven. You and I are not the judges. It does not fall to us to decide whether a man is saved. The Lord settles that question. I want to emphasize that **a justified man is a saved man, a man on his way to Heaven with all his sins put away.** II Peter 2:8 goes even further. It calls Lot a *righteous man.* Such language leaves us no room for saying anything else but that Lot is a saved man. He is a righteous man. II Peter 2:9 describes Lot with yet another word. *The Lord knoweth how to deliver the godly.* Now Lot was delivered from the judgment upon Sodom; therefore, these verses tell us, by inference, that Lot was a *godly* man. That means he is saved. Even as we see Lot's dwelling in wicked Sodom, the Scripture makes it very clear that Lot is a *justified* man; Lot is a *righteous* man; and Lot is a *godly* man.

Lot did not deserve to be saved.

Based upon Scripture, therefore, I can go so far as to say that Lot is actually a type of the believer! The believer can go in the wrong direction. He can get among the wrong company.

Lot represents the believer who is backslidden, careless towards the will of God, swallowed up by the world, and sorely chastened on account of his disobedience. But Lot is a saved man. Oh, I admit that there are times, perhaps all the time in your mind, when Lot does not look like a believer. He does not act like a child of God, and he does not speak like a child of God every time we find him in conversation. Given the way he finished up in that dreadful passage of Genesis 19, we might even add the words, "He does not deserve to be saved!" Let me quickly say that not one of us deserves mercy from God. Not one of us has been saved because of his own merit. The fact is that nobody deserves to be saved. Do you have hold of that? *Nobody.* You and I—and Lot—are saved because of the loving kindness of the Lord. We are saved because the mercy of God has kept us out of hell. That is all. Furthermore, there have been times when some of us, to our own shame, have acted such that we also did not appear to be God's people. Perhaps because of your sinful walk, someone may have put a question mark over your salvation. Which of us is without sin? Who can cast the first stone? Sadly, each of us has failed the Lord.

I say again that Lot is a type of the believer. As we look at this portion of the history of Lot's life, which is contained in Genesis chapters 13 to 19, we will be looking to him as an example—not as Abraham was an example for us to follow, but sadly, as an example for us to shun. Lot was a backslidden Christian. His example is important to warn us against the grievous sin of leaving God's fellowship, and his story will enable us to answer four important questions:

1. How does God deal with the backslider?
2. What weaknesses of the flesh can tempt us to get out of God's will?
3. What actions and circumstances of life can set us upon a downward slide?
4. What is the answer for the backslidden Christian?

Now we are dealing here with a real flesh-and-blood man. He actually walked this earth; he married, had children, ran a business, and lived among both believers and unbelievers. The lives of real people will not be categorized in neat boxes, and Lot's life will defy a theological outline. As we trace his steps, therefore, the answers to these questions will not be in perfect order. But the answers will be there. Look for them. May God use this study to teach us to avoid Lot's mistakes and to desire with all of our hearts to walk in the paths of righteousness.

Lot came under the chastening stroke of God's hand.

The New Testament account tells us that every day he lived in the city of Sodom, Lot's righteous soul was vexed with the filthy conversation of the wicked. It was an offence to him to see the deeds of the wicked and to hear the words they were saying. His righteous soul was stung, discouraged, grieved. The atmosphere of the wicked city of Sodom was depressive to Lot's spirit. This grieving of the soul in the presence of sin is a sign of conversion. The unhappiness a person feels when he is away from the Lord is a good indication that God has done a work in the man's soul. He may be in the wrong place, but he knows all the while these things are wrong, and he really wants no part of them. If you are born again, my friend, then you are spoiled for the world. You cannot live with peace of mind in the city of the wicked. **The Lord makes the backslider miserable.** I have good reason to believe that you are not saved if you call yourself a Christian and declare that you are away from God, that you are living in the world and like the world, and yet are happy and contented all the while. If you are not living now in the right place with God, and you are truly one of His, I think it true to say that the Lord will make you unhappy, terribly unhappy. He will give you no rest until you run back to the Saviour's feet. If you are like Lot, you are in the wrong place, you have no righteous business being where you are at the present moment, and—I can safely say—that your soul is vexed.

Perhaps you feel these words are harsh. These may not be the words you want to hear. But the Scripture has more to say about backsliding. The passage in I Corinthians 11:31-32, which is often read at the communion service, is quite clear. *For if we would judge ourselves, we should not be judged. But when we are judged, we are chastened of the Lord, that we should not be condemned with the world.* This passage is saying simply that God wants to separate His people from the world; therefore, when they backslide or become cold and hardened in heart and begin to wander away, if they would judge themselves at such a moment, they will not be judged by the Lord. God will not have to use the chastening rod when they judge themselves, and then He will be faithful to bring them back to repentance. The wayward Christian may try to be like the world, but God will not allow him to go on the way he has been living. God chastened Lot sorely, as our study will show. Lot lost everything God gave him. He may have prospered for a while, but God saw to it that he came to the place of complete poverty. God would not allow him to go on unchecked. **The Lord chastens the backslider.** Oh, dear believer, do you not see the great mercy and wisdom of the Lord in this case? Our dear Saviour will not let us go. Do you hear? He will not allow you to go on unchecked and unchastened. He must pull in the reins. He must pull you up to a standstill so that you will not be condemned with the world. He must show you, after all, that you are His child.

The lovingkindness of a faithful God.

Our faithful, wise and loving heavenly Father not only makes sure we cannot live happily out of fellowship with Him, He not only chastens us as His children when we are turned out of the way, but He does something even more wonderful when these actions do not bring us back to Him. **God delivers the backslidden child of God from his compromise.** The passage in II Peter gives us a statement of God's love and mercy towards the backslider: *And delivered just Lot, vexed with the filthy conversation of the wicked: (For that righteous man dwelling among them, in seeing and hearing, vexed his righteous soul from day to day with their unlawful deeds;) The Lord knoweth how to deliver the godly out of temptations, and to reserve the unjust unto the day of judgment to be punished.* God delivered Lot from the judgment upon Sodom. These verses cry, "Look at what God did for Lot. He delivered that man who was so unhappy in Sodom. God removed him from that place." Oh, let us pray that the Lord will get His people out of the place of compromise and ruin of soul. May the Lord bring His people out. The Lord has a great interest in redeeming His saints, and He will deliver the godly out of temptation, the Scriptures say. This is His will for you, dear wayward Christian. Call upon Him and He will answer you. If with all your heart you truly seek Him, you will most certainly find Him. Cry for deliverance, child of God. He is the Good Shepherd Who will restore your soul and put your feet back into the narrow path. Confess your faults to Him, for He is longsuffering, full of mercy, and ready to forgive.

> *Come, ye disconsolate, where'er ye languish,*
> *Come to the mercy seat, fervently kneel;*
> *Here bring your wounded hearts, here tell your anguish;*
> *Earth has no sorrows that heaven cannot heal.*

> *Joy of the desolate, light of the straying,*
> *Hope of the penitent, fadeless and pure!*
> *Here speaks the Comforter, tenderly saying,*
> *"Earth has no sorrows that heaven cannot cure."*

We may well wonder, given that he had such a good example in his Uncle Abraham, how Lot came to be in such sin and separation from God. Though Lot knew the Lord, he exhibited two weaknesses of the flesh that dogged him and dragged him downwards. Watch these things carefully, because they can afflict you as well.

First, **Lot was easily led**. I would call Lot a taken man.
That may sound like an odd label, but all throughout this
account, you see that Lot is *taken* here and there. Genesis 11:31:
*And Terah took Abram his son, and Lot the son of Haran his son's
son.* In the first instance, Terah took Lot away from Babylon.
Then he took him to the place called Haran, and from Haran,
Abraham took Lot to Canaan. Later on, Abraham took Lot
into Egypt. It seems that Lot resembles Mr. Pliable in *The
Pilgrim's Progress.* He is ready to go this way and that way,
wherever Abraham goes, or wherever Terah goes. It seems as
if Lot cannot use his own initiative except in the wrong way,
as when he goes to Sodom. Do we not see people all the time
who are easily led? And what is sad to me is that that they are
easily influenced to do wrong, but not so easily led to do right.
It seems to be a harder thing to lead them into the paths of
righteousness. So Lot is Scripture's Mr. Pliable. He is taken
here and he is taken there. It seems to me that Lot can go
anywhere. He does not have a character of his own. I wonder
if there is a reader here who can remember in his own history
where his backsliding began. Somebody took you to that place.
Do you remember it? You went along quite willingly. You were
easily led. You were a taken person. That is a sad thing. You
ought to have character enough not to be taken in the wrong
direction. You need to seek the Lord's leading for yourself and
follow Him. He alone can be your Guide, your Wisdom.

In the second place, **Lot was fascinated by the world.** Lot
pitched his tent toward Sodom. He seemed drawn towards the
place. That expression in Genesis 13:12 means that Lot was
going as far as he could away from the tents of prayer, and as
near as he could to the gates of Sodom without actually going
into the city. He was sliding towards sin and away from God's
fellowship. Read Jeremiah 2:13, 19. *For my people have committed
two evils; they have forsaken me the fountain of living waters, and
hewed them out cisterns, broken cisterns, that can hold no water.
Thine own wickedness shall correct thee, and thy backslidings shall
reprove thee: know therefore and see that it is an evil thing and bitter,*

that thou hast forsaken the LORD thy God, and that my fear is not in thee, saith the Lord GOD of hosts. God classifies backsliding as an evil and bitter thing. This is one of the key Scriptures about backsliding, so we need to take note of it. We have so many backsliders in these days. We hardly know whether some of them were ever saved. I am sure that in some cases there are false professions, but there are many children of God who are sliding into deeper and deeper sin, and further separation from the Lord. This is an evil thing and bitter. No one should say, "I am a backslider; therefore I can sin. I am backslidden; therefore I can do all sorts of things that Christians cannot do." God does not accept your backslidden state as an excuse for your sin. You are much more to blame in the sight of God if you sit back comforting yourself with the way you can live in sin and live for the world because you are a backslider. Perhaps you have lulled yourself into thinking that someday you will make things right, but right now, you have no heart for getting back to fellowship with God. You may even go to church and feel unconvicted. You may say, "Preach away, Preacher. Really lay it hard on those other Christians who are going on with God, but leave me out of it for I am a backslider." Well, if you really are a backslider, above all you need a word from God, or soon you will find out how evil and bitter a thing it is to be away from the Lord. Oh, you will soon lose your comfort in the state into which you have come.

Lot's backsliding was a progression of downward steps, one after the other. It is possible for the child of God to be on the downhill, step after step leading further away from blessing. We did notice the downward steps of Abraham as he went into Egypt. Then we saw the upward steps as he went back to Canaan, the Land of Promise. Listen, Christian. You need to be progressing upward. The Bible says, *The path of the just is as a shining light, that shineth more and more unto the perfect day.* The path grows lighter because it is climbing up towards the sun. The Christian should be growing in grace. Are you examining your steps to see whether in all these years since you were saved you have been progressing—progressing in

Bible reading, learning more and more about the Saviour, growing in a greater love for the Lord? We need to pray, "Lord, fill my heart with love for Thee. Lord, give me more joy in the things of God. Help me to love to pray and read Thy Word. Keep me near the cross. Keep me walking in the pathway of fellowship with Thee." This is a prayer that honours the Lord, and one that He will answer. When you pray, pray for your own soul, pray that you will grow in the things of the Lord.

Lot was a fool. He pitched his tent as far as he could away from the tents of prayer and as near as he could to the city without going into the gates of Sodom. You cannot play with sin. You cannot play with the devil and do well. Don't deceive yourself. If the downward marks are there all too clearly in your life, then it is about time that you awakened and recognized your danger. Don't play this game. The Lord is giving you a word, perhaps just in time, to save you from going on in your recklessness and folly. *Be not deceived; God is not mocked: for whatsoever a man soweth, that shall he also reap.*

When Lot left Abraham and headed towards Sodom, the Scripture tells us that he *dwelled in the cities of the plain.* How he could dwell there and not be able to dwell with Abraham is strange thing, but when the heart is not right, God's people put up with sin much more easily than they will put up with other Christians. They will find fault in God's house, and they will make excuses for the world. This was a foolish attitude on Lot's part. It was a step in his downward progression. His fascination with the world blinded his eyes to its dangers, and he went from pitching his tent towards Sodom to dwelling right in the plain where Sodom was situated. In those early days, Lot must have thought, "I could never *live* there. I must not, for I am a child of God. It would be wrong for me to live right in the city, but I can stay outside as long as I am near to the gate to do business."

You see, most times, a Christian does not backslide in a day; he does not abandon God in one step. When the devil engineers your downfall, everything happens over a period of time. You start going after the world in a small way. It draws you. You involve yourself in seemingly innocuous activities. You make this mistake, another blunder, yet another error, and sin is leading you down, down, down. It is as though you suddenly find yourself heading downhill faster and faster and you cannot find the brake. Oh, may God help you if you are on the downhill slide. May God open your eyes to it. Call for His help. Plead the blood over your soul. The Lord is able to stop your downward steps into sin.

The next thing we see is Lot *dwelling in Sodom*. Genesis 14:11 and 12 tell us that Lot suddenly found himself in trouble. Two confederations of kings went to war against each other in the valley of Siddim. The victors took a spoil of those cities and carried Lot and his goods away in the process. Abraham rescued Lot, who went back to live—in Sodom! By the time we get to Genesis 19 we learn that Lot continued to live in the wicked city. We can't help but ask, how did Lot come to actually dwell in such a place? Why did he stay there?

This question is especially pressing since we know that Lot never intended to live permanently in Sodom. We see this in Genesis 19:9. The men of the city knew that Lot had declared he would not stay, for they said, *This one fellow came in to sojourn.* Lot must have explained at the start, "I'm here temporarily; on no account would I *remain* in Sodom!" The backslider always has to make excuses for himself, explaining his sin, and justifying his failure.

But the slide continued. Eventually Lot *sat in the gate of Sodom*, a place of position and prominence. You see, he gained promotion. Lot not only continued to live in the city, but he began to take significant part in its activities. He had a post now like that of the Lord Mayor. There he saw things that he ought not to have seen. He heard things he ought not to have heard. How did Lot get to such a position? It certainly was not by accident. The devil saw to that. My friend, we need to stop here for a time. There are things we need to learn from

Lot. We will need to know the man a bit more intimately. Instead of standing off and judging him from afar, we want to get as close to him as we can and peer into his soul.

In the life of every Christian the devil can use difficulties, discouragements, and disasters to weaken him and influence him to make a foolish decision, or to head in a wrong direction. This is what happened to Lot. I would hasten to say here that God, on the other hand, always makes a way to escape from every temptation. Ultimately the responsibility for Lot's sin was on his own shoulders. God never allows His children to endure more temptation than they can bear; but if a Christian refuses to heed God's warnings and fails to ask for His help in time of need, he will step out of the place of God's blessing. Events came into Lot's life which influenced him to head away from Canaan and into the world; and because Lot was weak in character, that is he was easily led and quite fascinated by the world, he succumbed to these temptations. Listen, my dear friend, you need to submit your thinking to the Lord. You need to read His Word and meditate upon His great mercy and pardon and power to His children. He will strengthen your resolve, and enable you to gird up the loins of your mind so that you will not fall prey to every temptation that besets you.

The chickens come home to roost - Lot's past sins begin to catch up with him.

The first significant event in Lot's downward slide was the quarrel in the camp. **Lot quarrelled with his brethren.** Now if the devil can see to it that there is a falling-out between you and another believer, he will do that. The Christian needs to be on his toes. We need to recognize that there is an enemy. The arch-enemy of our souls is the devil, and even though we know what the Bible says about him, we still are caught napping much of the time. We come to our prayer meetings, our worship services, and other church functions as if the devil does not exist. Now I know there are some very respectable

Christians who want to tell us that the devil is already locked up and thrown into the bottomless pit where he will be for a thousand years. Perhaps this is the reason these folks discount the presence of Satan in the house of God. The devil is not in the bottomless pit yet. The devil is not bound for a thousand years at this time. That time is yet in the future. Foolishly, we come up to the house of God as if there were no devil. When a small bit of difficulty arises with another Christian, we don't have an awareness that the devil might fasten on that and use it. We are not guarding against the possibility of the devil's hand in that situation. We see only the problem as if it stood alone. A strife or a disagreement seems to be only that, and we are not watchful and sober. Rather, we need to think, "Satan could get in here and make a mountain out of a molehill. He could make havoc of the church. We must pray and walk closely with the Lord here, asking for His grace to bring us through without harm to the work of God." There is an adversary. There was a quarrel in the camp.

After this, Lot began to think about separating from Abraham. And the next event is recorded in Genesis 13:10. *And Lot lifted up his eyes, and beheld all the plain of Jordan, that it was well watered every where, before the LORD destroyed Sodom and Gomorrah, even as the garden of the LORD, like the land of Egypt, as thou comest unto Zoar.* This moment seems like a small event, but it contained an element in the process of getting Lot into Sodom. *Lot lifted up his eyes.* He cast about looking for a place away from Beth-el, the place of the altar. He looked *to the world* to find a place to get away from his difficulties. He was looking for an excuse to leave godly fellowship to find a place where he didn't have to deal with the problems he was facing!

Lot left the tents of prayer—the second step in his slide downward. That was a sad thing. He would have been far better leaving his herds. He reacted to trouble and strife in the wrong way. He thought that leaving Beth-el behind and going into the comfort of the world would solve his problems. He left the place where there was help and fellowship. Is it not strange how people blame the Lord when there is trouble? Perhaps you have been hurt. Perhaps you have had a setback in your life. You may have a heavy heart. Be very careful. Often the first thing people do at a time like that is to quit the prayer meeting. It is as though they are disgruntled toward God, so they stop praying. They stop meeting with God's people. It is a dreadful mistake to leave off praying with God's people. It is a very necessary means of grace, a means of upward progress, of sanctification in your soul. It is also a means of protection against the influence of the world. Listen, my friend, the time when you are hurt is the time when you need the prayer meeting. You need the Lord, you need His help, and you need the support of His people. Times of discouragement are never times to stay away. These are the times to attend the prayer meetings more faithfully than ever, for God Himself will meet you there.

A strange threesome - Sodom, Egypt and Eden.

And Lot lifted up his eyes, and beheld all the plain of Jordan, that it was well watered every where, before the LORD destroyed Sodom and Gomorrah, even as the garden of the LORD, like the land of Egypt. Here we notice three locations: Sodom, Egypt and Eden. Eden's garden—Lot did not see any difficulty in likening Sodom to Paradise. Up there in the mountains, he scanned the length and breadth of the Land of Promise with Abraham. It seemed all the same to Lot. He could say, "Do you know that place down there is really green and lush. It looks to me like the Garden of Eden." Then the Scripture adds the words, "It was really like Egypt." Those are words you want to think about.

From that distance, the plain of the cities must have seemed like a heaven on earth. Everything looked green and lush, orderly, prosperous, attractive. But really, down there in the valley, inside those walls of the city of Sodom, it was a den of wickedness. It was hell let loose. It was anything but a paradise on earth. Many people are fooled by the world, especially the young. Young Christians can be misled by worldly places and opportunities, and think they have got a kind of paradise before them. How dreadfully foolish! They are making the same mistake that Lot made. You cannot bring these two different worlds together. It was like Paradise, yet it was like the land of Egypt. Why should Egypt be brought into the text?

The fact is, after Abraham took Lot to Egypt, though he got Lot out of Egypt, he never got Egypt out of Lot. Lot could not forget Egypt; he liked it there. He liked the lifestyle. He liked the ungodly atmosphere. He liked the money. He liked to have all that there was in the world, because in Egypt he had found plenty, wealth and comfort. Egypt had a very high standard of civilization. Lot liked all the comforts that came with it. There were the carpets, for example. It was a bit different from living in an old battered tent out in the wilderness. He got tired of the sand and the stones and the dirt, and remembered how luxurious Egypt had been. It was beautiful. It was sophisticated. It was interesting—fascinating. It was really living! And it was Abraham who took him there.

The marks of the world and the stains of sin which can never be blotted out from the mind.

Some of you go to places where you should not go. I think also that you take people there with you, and you do not think what you are doing. You could be laying the foundation for somebody's ruin. Abraham took Lot to Egypt and he never got over it. Lot never got Egypt out of his soul, and one of the reasons he chose the city of Sodom was that it looked like Egypt. What a sad chapter! Child of God, perhaps you can see yourself pictured in this account. Be careful about your influence. If you take somebody where you should not be, or direct them into an activity in which you should not take part, take sober heed what you do. You may be wise enough— although I doubt it—you may be wise enough to get yourself out, but what about that other poor soul? What have you done? You have really helped to drag that poor soul down into ruin. Our Lord made the matter quite clear in Matthew 18:6, 7. *But whoso shall offend one of these little ones which believe in me, it were better for him that a millstone were hanged about his neck, and that he were drowned in the depth of the sea. Woe unto the world because of offences! for it must needs be that offences come; but woe to that man by whom the offence cometh!*

There were three who went into Egypt: Abraham, Sarah and Lot. These three were never the same again. If ever anything speaks a truth plainly, this account does. You cannot backslide, you cannot break fellowship with God and get out of His will, and be the same as before. Sin leaves scars; it leaves memories. Sometimes it leaves shipwrecked lives. Abraham exposed Lot to Egypt and he never got over it. He developed a liking for Egypt and was no longer the man he was before. Abraham endangered his own life and marriage, and put his wife in a dangerous situation when he went down into Egypt. How many are there who have nearly wrecked their homes because they have played about with the world? Abraham got richer—at least he added to his riches—and learned how to lie. And while they were in Egypt, Sarah got Hagar, the woman who broke her heart and who nearly broke her home.

Perhaps you have got a liking for some of the glitter of the world. It could be that on some occasion you went to a banquet where everybody took wine. You were under pressure to take just one glass. Perhaps you came out all right, but many a drunkard has begun with just such a situation. Every alcoholic began with one glass. You talk more easily and fit in better. Oh yes, drink the cup—you will find the dregs at the bottom. All that the world has to offer will sting in the end. And your influence for good, for Christ, will be compromised.

At the moment Lot lifted up his eyes to look toward Sodom, he had returned from Egypt to Canaan with Abraham, and was dwelling at Beth-el, the place of the altar. He was where fellowship was had with the God of Abraham; yet he cast his eyes on the world. He was at the house of God (that is the meaning of Beth-el), and even there Lot lifted up his eyes and saw the cities of the plain. How many have sat in church on the Lord's Day morning with a Bible in their hands. They have looked every inch like Christians, but all the while they have sat in the house of God with their minds focused on the world—fascinated. It is just as well the preacher never guessed it. Lot lifted up his eyes to gaze toward the world.

The blight of self-will.

As we follow Lot's downward slide, the events that brought Lot to actually dwell in the wicked city of Sodom, we now come to the moment of his tragic choice. Genesis 13:11, *Then Lot chose him all the plain of Jordan.* Do you see the unusual wording? Lot chose him. Why is the word him placed in the sentence? Why not just, *Then Lot chose all the plain of Jordan*? The wording is to convey that Lot chose for himself. He had only his own wishes in mind; he did not seek the mind of the Lord in the matter. There is no mention of prayer here; Lot did not build an altar and pray, "Now Lord, Abraham has allowed me to turn to the right or to the left. Lord, what should I do? What way would You have me to go?" No, Lot would not build an altar. Lot would not pray. *In all thy ways acknowledge him, and he shall direct thy paths.* Lot knew nothing about the Lord's direction in choosing a way to go. He chose for himself. The fact was, **he took a step in his life without asking God's will.** And such a step is always a step down.

Is that not the story of shipwreck? Is that not the preamble for disaster? Lot chose for himself. There are thousands of Christians doing the same thing, men and women who ought to know better. *In all thy ways acknowledge him, and he shall direct thy paths.* How lovingly our heavenly Father offers His guidance. How necessary it is to seek God's will. How well we know this verse! We need to pray for wisdom at all times— whether it be for a little thing or a great thing— enough wisdom to acknowledge the Lord in all our ways. Lot chose for himself. Oh Lot, stop! Get to the altar. Seek forgiveness for your rebellion. Ask for the Lord's guidance. Oh, don't leave the camp without the Lord's being with you. But Lot would not seek God. Take your pen and write in the margin beside Genesis 13:11, "Lot chose for himself." This is the sense of the reading, and we must never forget how failure to acknowledge the Lord added one more step to Lot's progress towards Sodom.

Lured by the prosperity and the "bright lights".

But Lot was to continue on in his foolishness. Next, he decided to look for the means to improve his lifestyle. Of course, Lot wanted to better himself; and although he determined never to go *into* Sodom, Lot reasoned that he would have a ready market for all his flocks if he did business *nearby*. Remember all those flocks and herds, all the cattle that he had for multitude? Why would a man have all that stock and produce if he did not have a market? Of course, he needed a market. He might have reasoned, "There is not much of a market up there in the hills with Abraham so very far away from the best of the trade. I need to make more money. Down in Sodom and the neighbouring cities of the plain with their vast populations, there is a ready market for the flocks that I have. The citizens of Sodom need my produce, and I shall be able to make a better profit by selling to city people." Soon, because of his business dealings, Lot became a known figure in the city. His business was established and he gained promotion. He became a wealthy, prominent man. Now there is nothing wrong with prospering in business, provided we do right. God gives us the means to work hard and keep the labours of our hands. But **Lot decided he had to go deeper into the world in order to make a little more money. He was not content with all the wealth he had with Abraham back in Canaan.** Discontent always sets us on a downward slide.

Lot had it all worked out. He would never go into Sodom. He would just profit from the people of Sodom. But, I have to say, the world is a place of change. Lot forgot that. And he forgot about the devil. He would go down on market days and play around with Sodom, but he would never go in. He would play around with the devil but he would never be caught. What a fool he was! If you are playing with fire you need to revise your thinking. You need to stay away from that fire. You need to be as far away from it as you can get. Lot didn't bargain on the devil. Satan meant to get Lot into Sodom. Believers may find themselves in the same situation. Take out the word *Sodom* and insert instead the word *sin*. Or try adding the word *trouble*. The meaning is the same: Satan means to get Christians into sin. He intends to bring them into trouble, especially if they are playing around with fire. It is as if Lot is smiling at the devil, saying, "I know too much about you, boy. You can't get me. I can actually go down to the gates of Sodom and do business and take the money of your crowd there, and you will never draw me into it. Abraham has taught me all about the world. I know too much. Catch me in Sodom? You will never get me into it."

How the devil got Lot into Sodom - in spite of a strong determination not to go into it.

As I said, the world is a place of change. Circumstances change, and unless you have the Lord in your life, leading you and walking with you, you can never tell what tomorrow will bring. God help that man who, while a Christian, is still living in the world as if he were a worldly man, without prayer, without the Bible, without seeking God. You cannot get by alone. Change came to Lot suddenly; it was a disaster. Genesis 14:2 tells us that a war started, and this drastic change of events *forced Lot to flee into the city* for refuge. Lot was shoehorned into Sodom by events that he never foresaw. **Lot was unprepared for disaster because he had deserted the tents of prayer and left himself wide open on the plains where**

there was no protection. He was too far away to get back before disaster struck. He ran into Sodom. Thereafter, he never got away from the place without carrying the stain of it on his soul.

You cannot laugh at the devil. You cannot play fast and loose with sin. The devil is stronger than you are and the events of life are not under your control. You need to be in the right place when difficulties appear. War came and suddenly Lot could not stay in the plain where the battles raged; he did what he said he would never do, in order to avoid being killed. I don't know what he did with the herds, whether he got them into the city or not. But it is quite clear that Lot's whole life changed from that moment on, and we know that he apologetically explained his intention, when he sought a dwelling there. He said it was for only a short time, "just temporary, you see." Only for the time being. So he used the word *sojourn*. And once he was in, that was it.

Once the devil has you in the snare, it is going to be next to impossible to get out of it. You cannot close your ear to God and to His Word. You cannot pretend that because you are a backslider you can do what you like. You cannot control circumstances. You cannot win over the devil without the power of God. You are weak and foolish and needy. Do not leave the place of safety, the place of the altar where you will hear the sweet voice of the Saviour declaring His love that He has had for you from before the foundation of the world. Child of God, how can we think the world has anything to offer, when our Saviour, our Friend, has given us all things to enjoy? Can anything or anyone compare to such love?

> *Jesus has loved me—wonderful Saviour!*
> *Jesus has loved me, I cannot tell why;*
> *He came to rescue sinners unworthy;*
> *My heart He conquered, for Him I would die.*
>
> *Jesus has saved me—wonderful Saviour!*
> *Jesus has saved me, I cannot tell how;*
> *But this I do know, He came, my ransom,*
> *Dying on Calv'ry with thorns on His brow.*

Jesus will lead me—wonderful Saviour!
Jesus will lead me, I cannot tell where,
So I will follow thru joy or sorrow,
Sunshine or tempest, since He leads me there.

So we see that actions and events which were part of a wilful, backslidden life, only served to draw Lot inexorably into the most wicked city of his day. These downward steps will appear in the life of any Christian who is not on guard. Does any reader see himself in this story? Learn the lessons well. Do not make Lot's mistakes.

1. Lot quarreled with his brethren.
2. Lot left the tents of prayer.
3. Lot made a choice without asking God's direction.
4. Lot was not content with God's provision.
5. Lot looked to the world for a more comfortable life style.
6. Lot found himself in the wrong place when disaster struck.

Lot stayed so long in Sodom that there came a time when the Lord had to send His angels to stir the man. God was going to judge the city, but Lot sat in the city gate. He was sitting there when the messengers of God came to bring him out. "Get up, man. This is the last night Sodom will ever have." Oh, the mercy of God. Lot did not deserve such mercy. There are Christians who are just sitting down contentedly, letting things roll on. God is saying, "Child of God, get up. Don't be sitting there. Get up now! Flee this place." The Lord wanted Lot to get up because He had an interest in Lot's own ungodly friends and family as well. Lot was instructed to warn them to flee judgment. There are Christians who think that God does not care about the ungodly. Well, He does. Otherwise you would not have been saved. You were saved while you were yet in your sin, while you were a poor, ungodly, unclean, depraved wretch.

The terrible price of unjudged sin.

Remember how God treats backsliders? He makes them miserable and he chastens them. Oh, the chastening rod was heavy on Lot. He lost nearly everything in Sodom. That is what sin does to Christians who try to live in the world. Lot lost his peace, suffering vexation everyday he was there. He lost his children, and some of them actually perished in the overthrow. He lost his wife; she looked back and never saw another thing. He lost his wealth. He lost his walk with the Lord. He never built an altar; he never offered any sacrifice once, not once with all the herds he had. You cannot read in the Scripture record that Lot sacrificed one lamb for the Lord. He lost his herds. Finally he had no herds to look after. You have to be careful that you do not get too busy. It may be if you get too busy and have no time for Him, that the Lord will have to see to it that you will not be so busy after all.

> *Room for pleasure, room for business,*
> *But for Christ the Crucified,*
> *Not a place that He can enter,*
> *In the heart for which He died?*

So the time came when Lot did not have any herds. He lost his home. He ended up living in a cave. He may have accumulated so much wealth in Sodom that he was able to live in a mansion in the city—but he was reduced to living outdoors in a cave. He lost his influence. The Bible says that the men of the city and his own children mocked him. He lost his testimony, for he fell into drunkenness and gross sin. He lost his fellowship with God. He lost his joy.

But we must hasten to insert the reminder that God mercifully delivered Lot from judgment. He was saved. Remember, **God not only chastens, but he delivers.** God was faithful to his own, even when that child threw away every advantage and blessing which God had given him. Truly, in the words of II Peter 2, *the Lord knoweth how to deliver the godly* *out of temptations.* Sadly, the Old Testament never mentions Lot again. He just fades out of Scriptural history without any good comment at all. Abraham's nephew—the backslider. Let us learn these lessons well. The world will rob you of every blessing. The way of the world is a downward path. You don't have to walk that path, my Christian friend. God has made a way to escape. He has saved you from the world. If you have fallen prey to its allure, if you have slumbered in its comforts, heed the merciful call of God. Get up now. Flee to the Saviour. This is the answer to a backslidden life.

> *God calling yet! Shall I not hear?*
> *Earth's pleasures shall I still hold dear?*
> *Shall life's swift passing years all fly,*
> *And still my soul in slumber lie?*
>
> *God calling yet! Shall I not rise?*
> *Can I His loving voice despise,*
> *And basely His kind care repay?*
> *He calls me still—can I delay?*
>
> *God calling yet! And shall He knock,*
> *And I my heart the closer lock?*
> *He still is waiting to receive,*
> *And shall I dare His Spirit grieve?*
>
> *God calling yet! And shall I give*
> *No heed, but still in bondage live?*
> *I wait, but He does not forsake;*
> *He calls me still—my heart, awake!*
>
> *God calling yet! I cannot stay;*
> *My heart I yield without delay:*
> *Vain world, farewell, from thee I part;*
> *The voice of God hath reached my heart.*

CHAPTER SIX

AFTER THESE THINGS - ABRAHAM'S REWARD

" And the LORD said unto Abram, after that Lot was separated from him, Lift up now thine eyes. . .all the land which thou seest, to thee will I give it, and to thy seed for ever. . .Then Abram removed his tent, and came and dwelt in the plain of Mamre, which is in Hebron, and built there an altar unto the LORD. And it came to pass . . .That these made war with Bera king of Sodom. . .And when Abram heard that his brother was taken captive, he. . .pursued. . .And he brought back all the goods, and also brought again his brother Lot. . .And the king of Sodom went out to meet him after his return. . .And Melchizedek king of Salem brought forth bread and wine: and he was the priest of the most high God. And he blessed him, and said, Blessed be Abram of the most high God. . . And he gave him tithes of all. And the king of Sodom said unto Abram. . .take the goods to thyself. And Abram said. . .I will not take any thing that is thine, lest

thou shouldst say, I have made Abram rich. . .After these things the word of the LORD came unto Abram in a vision, saying, Fear not, Abram: I am thy shield, and thy exceeding great reward. **//**

Genesis 13:14-15:1

THERE IS ALWAYS AN AFTERWARDS to every circumstance in life. There is an afterwards for the man who does wrong, as Lot did—and we saw the severity of chastisement which came after Lot's backsliding. There is also an afterwards for the man who pleases God, as Abraham did. In all the difficulties which afflicted Abraham after his return to Canaan, he sought to obey God and the Lord rewarded him greatly.

Note the words which appear here for the first time in the Bible.

This section of Scripture is distinguished by several occurrences of *first mentions*, that is, words or phrases which occur for the very first time in the Bible.

(a) As you have read prophecies of men such as Jeremiah and Ezekiel, you must have come across phrases such as *and there came the word of the Lord.* We call this phrase *a prophetic formula.* Genesis 15:1 is the first time this prophetic formula occurs: *After these things the word of the LORD came unto Abram.* Remember, Abraham had returned to the right place with God. When Abraham was restored to that rightful place of fellowship with God, the word of the Lord came to his soul with power and meaning. Dear believer, if you are in fellowship with the Lord, you too may expect to hear a word from God. Before you commence your daily reading of the Bible, start with prayer. **When you read the Scriptures with a prayerful heart from day to day, God will speak to your soul with power and meaning,** just as He spoke to Abraham. Each time we open the Scriptures, we should earnestly ask, "Lord, speak to me; reveal Thyself to me today through the reading of Thy Word." Let us never take the reading of the Bible to be a chore, as if each day's study is just a duty to get through, speeding up the reading as we get nearer to the end, and thankfully closing the Bible for another day! Don't let your Bible reading be like that. Expect better things.

Lord, speak to me, that I may speak
In living echoes of Thy tone;
As Thou hast sought, so let me seek
Thy erring children lost and lone.

O teach me, Lord, that I may teach
The precious things thou dost impart;
And wing my words, that they may reach
The hidden depths of many a heart.

(b) In Genesis 15:1, the word *vision* occurs for the first time: *the word of the LORD came unto Abram in a vision.* In Abraham's time there was no such thing as a printed copy of the Scriptures. The book of Genesis was not available, nor Exodus, Leviticus, Deuteronomy, nor Samuel, Judges, Isaiah, nor the Psalms, never mind the New Testament. It was necessary for the Lord to speak and work in unusual ways with His saints. God was always faithful to speak to His people and to guide them through the words of prophecy and by the giving of visions. Today we have the Book, which is complete, forever settled in Heaven. It contains all that we need to know of God's mind and will for the believer. Today we expect God to speak by the Scriptures and not by visions. It behoves us, therefore, to pay responsible attention to the words of Holy Scripture.

The Christian must be guided in every part of life by the written Word of God. Do you want a vision of the precious Lord Jesus Christ? He is revealed, not by statues that cry, nor by healers and diviners; He is revealed by the Holy Spirit within the pages of Holy Writ. There are those who do not accept the completeness of the Bible, and who advise you to run helter-skelter after this one and that one who claim to have visions and who talk about words of knowledge, utterances in tongues, and so-called prophecies which are outside the ambit of Scripture. All of this is of the flesh and is likely, very likely, to lead the child of God into shipwreck and disaster. Remember that the Holy Spirit Himself works all the time within the periphery of Scripture. That means you and I, as ordinary mortals, have to stick to the written Word without any thought of departing from it. Never be tempted to add to, subtract from, or otherwise abandon the written Word of God, no matter how wise or inspiring someone else's "prophecy" may sound. Abraham listened for God's Word to him; you must do the same, if you would know blessing, fellowship and guidance.

(c) For your encouragement, Genesis 15:1 is also the location of the first *fear not* in Scripture. Oh, how the believer needs to hear these words from the Lord in many instances of life. How comforting they are to his soul! God has told us that He has not given us the spirit of fear, but of a sound mind. Today there is much fear abroad—fear of nuclear disaster, fear of violence, fear of poverty, fear of plague and disease. But God says over and over in Scripture, *Fear not, for I am thy God.* Many things could be said about the *fear nots* of the Bible, but this is the first mention of them. It comes at a very important time for Abraham, as we shall consider later.

(d) This same verse is also the first time that the words shield and reward occur in the Bible. We note that the Lord

Himself has become Abraham's *shield*, and Abraham's *reward*. How much Abraham needs to hear this welcome word, having passed through a serious time of testing. He has returned from Egypt, having battled the **world**. He has also battled the *flesh*, for in Chapter 13 the battle breaks out between the herdsmen of Abraham and the herdsmen of Lot, resulting in a very serious division. Chapter 14 describes Abraham in warfare again—pitched in and around the area of Sodom—battling the *devil*. These are vital chapters in Abraham's life, and how mercifully the Lord Himself comes to Abraham after these things and declares Himself to be all that Abraham needs. Have you come through difficult days, my friend? The Lord Himself will meet every need. Look to Him.

Be Thou my Vision, O Lord of my heart—
Nought be all else to me, save that Thou art;
Thou my best thought, by day or by night—
Waking or sleeping, Thy presence my light.

Be Thou my Wisdom, and Thou my true Word—
I ever with Thee and Thou with me, Lord;
Thou our great Father, I Thy true son—
Thou in me dwelling, and I with Thee one.

Riches I heed not, nor man's empty praise—
Thou mine inheritance, now and always;
Thou and Thou only, first in my heart—
High King of heaven, my Treasure Thou art.

It is necessary for us to pay heed to the precise time when God spoke to Abraham.

Genesis 15:1 clearly refers to a specific time—*After these things*. Abraham has passed through many periods of crisis. After the unhappy and disastrous journey into Egypt and the restoration of communion with God at the altar, after the strife with Lot which forced Abraham to admit that Lot was a thorn in his side instead of a source of encouragement and help, after the painful separation from Lot whom Abraham had considered as a son, after the dangerous rescue following the battle of the kings—*After these things—the word of the LORD came unto Abram in a vision, saying, Fear not, Abram: I am thy shield and thy exceeding great reward.* The Lord can give the believer encouragement, even after a time of personal grief. You will notice that Abraham found this word of encouragement coming to him from the Lord after he had fought the Lord's battles. Abraham, in chapter 14, had gone to rescue Lot, unworthy as his nephew was. Abraham put himself at risk, pursuing and overcoming the powerful foe, Chedorlaomer and his confederates. God was faithful, and he gave Abraham the victory.

What it means to have the Lord as our shield.

But victory has her own enemies. It might have been, after Abraham returned with the spoils of war, that the thought came to his mind, "Now there will be a reprisal. These mighty armies will come from the east in overwhelming numbers, looking for revenge. I am a wanted man. I will never be able to escape from them. I will certainly perish." This would most likely be Abraham's state of mind. Yet, after the battle had ended, the Lord came to His follower with a word of comfort: "Fear not, Abraham, I am thy shield. I am here, standing by you." What a word! That shield was Christ Himself offering protection to Abraham for the rest of his days. Remember, Abraham was in the enemy's territory. He could have perished at any time from the hand of the enemy. He was a man who needed protection, who needed a shield. He needed that shield to keep him alive.

We don't half realize the power of the devil, nor are we half aware of the danger which the Christian runs from day to day. I am convinced that not one Christian would be alive five minutes in the world were it not for the protection of the blood of Christ. *I am thy shield.* This title of the Lord reminds us of what we have been saved from. Though you may face dangers on the road, or dangers around the home, or dangers on the public scene, you may say with full assurance, "The Lord is my shield; the Lord will look after me everyday." The reason you remain alive in a world that is the devil's domain, where the strong man keeps his goods with power, is that the greater power of God has kept you. You are a witness to His salvation, and the Lord has kept this witness in a wicked world. The Lord has been our shield. He has kept us alive. By definition, a shield is something that is held between a soldier and the enemy, and that deflects blows from head or body. What a picture of Christ, our Mediator, the One Who stands between, Who intervenes in our behalf. His blood avails for us. It answers the wrath of God. It deflects the blows that we deserve. We plead that precious blood in every danger. It is reserved in Heaven for us, the redeemed of the Lord. There is power in the blood of the Lamb!

Jesus, Thy blood and righteousness
My beauty are, my glorious dress;
'Midst flaming worlds, in these arrayed,
With joy shall I lift up my head.

Following the victorious rescue operation, Abraham not only faced physical danger, but he faced a spiritual challenge which threatened to undo his resolve to leave all for Christ. Victory not only has her enemies, she herself may act the part of the enemy. Following a triumph, the believer is often besieged by great temptation. In Genesis 14, after the rescue of Lot, The King of that wicked city of Sodom went out to meet Abraham. The Bible tells us a marvelous fact: the Lord intervened with a special meeting with Abraham right at that time. *And the king of Sodom went out to meet him after his return. . . .And Melchizedek king of Salem brought forth bread and wine: and he was the priest of the most high God. And he blessed him, and said, Blessed be Abram of the most high God,*

possessor of heaven and earth: And blessed be the most high God
which hath delivered thine enemies into thy hand. And he gave him
tithes of all.

The reward granted at the appearing of the king.

I believe that when Abraham met the One called
Melchizedek, He was looking into the eyes of his Saviour. Some
good men would argue against that view. They say that
Melchizedek was a *type* of Christ. There is room for both
opinions. Certainly, whatever Melchizedek's identity, his
appearance came at an important juncture in Abraham's
experience. For our purposes here, however, I wish to consider
this personage a pre-incarnate appearance of Christ Himself.

This passage tells us that Melchizedek was a king, a priest,
and a prophet who brought Abraham the message of blessing
from God. Only Christ Himself ever held all the offices of
Prophet, Priest, and King. Further, Hebrews 7 indicates that
this King *was without father, without mother, without descent,*
having neither beginning of days, nor end of life; but made like unto
the Son of God. The passage also teaches that this Melchizedek
continually abides as a priest. The name *Melchizedek* means
literally, *King of Righteousness.* This same chapter calls Him
the *King of Peace.* Only One is eternal, and like unto the Son of
God, only One is the King of Righteousness and the King of
Peace, only One is a Priest forever—The very Christ of God.
Abraham met with One made like unto the Son of God—face
to face!

This Melchizedek reminded Abraham, that his victory had
been given him of God: *And blessed be the most high God, which*
hath delivered thine enemies into thy hand. The Bible then says
that Abraham gave tithes of all that he had to this King. Some
people might remark, "What an astounding thing for Abraham
to know about tithing! What a remarkable thing that Abraham
should give Him the tithe, and that it would be the tithes of
all! He tithed everything." But Abraham had met with the
Lord. He had been brought face to face with the reality that

the victory and the blessing were the Lord's. Clearly, Abraham's response was, "God has given me the means to obtain what I have. I could never have had the least of all these possessions if it had not been for the abounding goodness of God. And He has given me an astonishing victory in which I have been able to recover my nephew and all he possesses. How can I do any less than return Him the tenth, to acknowledge His magnificence, to return in a tangible way my thanksgiving to Him? I will honour Him with my tithe."

The message of the tithe.

Sometimes a Christian will say, "Must I really give a tithe? Does the Lord expect me to give a tenth to Him?" This has to be a question from one who has not yet realized that all that he is, all that he has, and all that he has been saved from and to, come solely from the hand of his God. God has loved us with an everlasting love, He has given us all things in Christ, He has given Himself. How can a tithe be enough to honour Him? What a great opportunity that God gives us to express our gratitude.

Tithing is a Biblical command which should be seen as a privilege and a wise ordinance given by God:

1. **Tithing is proportionate.** The tenth is the same to the man who is not so well off as to the man who is better off. It is the best way to give. Each one can, in a regular way, give to the work of the Lord.

2. **Tithing is proper.** It is a proper response by one who recognizes that God is the Giver of all. It gives the Christian a good opportunity to deal with the covetousness of his heart in a very practical way.

3. **Tithing is prompt.** I Corinthians 16:2 *Upon the first day of the week* we are to set aside as God has prospered us those gifts that are for His work. Why the first day of the week? Does not the Lord know our hearts? If we were to leave the tithe to the last day, it would become much more

difficult to give the tithe. The longer you hold on to it, the harder it is to part with it. This Scripture philosophy is right. It is just a simple way of saying, "Put the Lord Jesus first in your giving." When you think of your allocation of money and goods for the week, give the Lord His portion first. On the first day of the week, remember that Scriptural admonition, *seek ye first the kingdom of God, and his righteousness.* Certainly it makes good sense to say that if the Lord must be first in all things, then He must come first in our giving.

Learn to prove the Lord in your giving. You will never out-give the Lord. As God has honoured you, so you can honour Him. He does say, *them that honour me I will honour.* May the Lord give us grace to follow Abraham in the giving of tithes to our great King.

A refusal of the devil's rewards.

How gracious the Lord was to intervene with such a special meeting, for Abraham immediately faced a temptation. Abraham had to say no. Genesis 14:21-23 says, *And the king of Sodom said unto Abram, Give me the persons, and take the goods to thyself. And Abram said to the king of Sodom, I have lift up mine hand unto the LORD, the most high God, the possessor of heaven and earth, That I will not take from a thread even to a shoelatchet, and that I will not take any thing that is thine, lest thou shouldst say, I have made Abram rich.* The king of Sodom offered Abraham the spoils of battle, but he recognized some of those as belonging to the royal house of Sodom, and to the markets of that city. Abraham certainly had a right to the all the spoils of battle. He could have said to the king of Sodom, newly appointed as he was, "I went forward to the battle. You did not gather an army, and you did not go to the place of conflict. I went to the battle line, I risked my life, I fought with the enemy. The prize won in war is rightly mine." But Abraham did not even entertain such thoughts. He said no to all the spoils that were duly his.

Why did Abraham do such a thing? Because he did not want one thing that had the stamp of Sodom. We can watch him after the battle, as he carefully divides his possessions from those of the city of Sodom. He turns over a golden vase, but on the base of it is stamped "Made in Sodom." He hastily pushes it away. The Lord does not want him to have one thing tainted with the hallmark of Sodom. He picks up a soldier's shoe, but recognizes the lace as one made in Sodom. He throws it back on the heap. He will not take even the smallest item, neither a shoelatchet nor a thread from Sodom's possessions. Abraham certainly lives the life of a separated man. He provides us the example of a man apart from all the rest, a man dedicated to the Lord, a man who doesn't want one thing in his possession that is the world's. The Christian has to learn to say no to some things. The Christian must beware lest he gather baggage in the world. Listen, if there is anything in your life that in some sense has the stamp of Sodom on it, you don't want that in your possession. Do not keep anything at all which is vexing to the Lord. If the Lord shows you that what you have is not right, for His sake, indeed for your own sake, get rid of it. Push it away. It has no place. Have you grasped after the world, its things, its activities? This is the way to begin drifting from the path of righteousness. Oh, do not keep in your possession the accursed thing. It will bring you down.

Abraham's example speaks even further. Not only does he not want in his possession what God has cursed, but he wants nothing that is not *wholly* the Lord's. Would it not be wonderful if in our *own* experience we could be so dedicated to the Lord that we could truly consider all we possess to be the Lord's? Perhaps you have obtained a beautiful new car, shining and in showroom condition. It would be worthwhile to say, "Lord, use this car. Don't let it be solely my possession." The Lord will surprise you in how that car could be used for Him. What about your home? The Lord can use that in a great way to be a blessing to others and to bring honour to Him. Consider all God's blessings as His, and let there not be one thing, down to the least, that you do not give to Him. The Lord is no man's debtor. You cannot give to Him and lose out.

The Lord Himself is the best reward the believer can have.

After Abraham met the King, after he paid the tithe, after he said no to the world—*after these things*—he was none the poorer, because the Lord declared, *I am thy shield, and thy exceeding great reward.* God's titles always speak to His children; they declare how faithful and loving God is to us. Just as the title *shield* speaks to us of what we have been saved *from*, so the title *reward* speaks to us of what we have been saved to. The Lord has not only saved me from death and destruction, but He has promised me great blessings. Can you begin to think what it means for the Christian to have such a reward as this? God is saying, "Abraham, no matter how much you seem to have lost, I am your reward. Remember the time of the quarrel with Lot, when you allowed Lot to choose for himself the richly endowed plains of Jordan? He had the choice of the best of the land. Well, Abraham, you did not lose a thing. Do you remember that time when the king of Sodom approached you to bargain for the spoils, and you allowed him to take them all just for the sake of your testimony? Well, Abraham, you did not lose a thing. I am thy exceeding great reward, for anything that you have lost I will restore.

Peter asked the Lord, *Behold, we have forsaken all, and followed thee; what shall we have therefore?* And the precious Lord Jesus, Who would give up His glory, endure the hatred of those men He created, bear the sins of His own, bow under the wrath of His Father, shed His blood, and give His life, did not utter a word of reproach. Instead, He gave a word for Peter and for us all, *And every one that hath forsaken houses, or brethren, or sisters, or father, or mother, or wife, or children, or lands, for my name's sake, shall receive an hundredfold, and shall inherit everlasting life.* Is there a child of God who would say, "I have lost this and I have lost that in life. Do you know how important that is to me?" Perhaps one grieving soul would say, "Since the day I lost my wife, life has not been the same." Someone else may say, "I lost my business and my home. I lost everything." Maybe you feel that things are not the same now as you come to the house of God. My friend, it is tremendously important that you get hold of this verse, Fear not. . .*I am thy shield, and thy exceeding great reward.* Dwell on this truth. You have the Lord; you have His very Word. You have the Holy Spirit dwelling in your heart, your Guide and Comforter, Who will never leave you nor forsake you. You have the riches of His grace, and a new life, free from the curse and power of sin. You have the opportunity of Christian fellowship, the sweetness of social interaction with God's people that will edify and enrich you, unlike the friends of the world. You have the house of prayer, where you may lift up your heart to the Lord with others of like precious faith. You have the Friend Who sticks closer than a brother, who is touched with the feelings of your infirmities. You have your Creator, now your Redeemer, Who has restored Paradise and Who is preparing a place for you to dwell with Him for all eternity. Oh, think on these things, my friend. Our knowledge of the Lord should increase. Our dependence upon the Lord should increase. Our fellowship with the Lord should become closer and more intimate in these days. We need to seek the Lord, and ask that this promise will come home to us with great power, as it did to Abraham.

O soul, are you weary and troubled?
No light in the darkness you see?
There's light for a look at the Saviour,
And life more abundant and free!

His word shall not fail you—He promised;
Believe Him, and all will be well:
Then go to a world that is dying,
His perfect salvation to tell!

Turn your eyes upon Jesus,
Look full in His wonderful face;
And the things of earth will grow strangely dim
In the light of His glory and grace.

How Abraham applied the Word of God to his heart and turned it into a remarkable prayer.

Fear not, Abram: I am thy shield, and thy exceeding great reward. We know that this wonderful promise gripped Abraham's very soul, for the patriarch immediately asked, *Lord GOD, what wilt thou give me?* Is this not a word to our own souls? Abraham was always looking for new experiences, and if the Lord gave him a promise, he was the first to say, "Lord, will you make it good?" He was not content to have just the promise, he was looking for the experience of it too. And what promises God gave! *And he brought him forth abroad, and said, Look now toward heaven, and tell the stars, if thou be able to number them: and he said unto him, So shall thy seed be. . . .In the same day the LORD made a covenant with Abram saying, Unto thy seed have I given this land, from the river of Egypt unto the great river, the river Euphrates.* As we follow Abraham through his pilgrimage, we see that the Lord fulfilled all His word to this man who proved God in such a powerful way. Child of God, seek to follow in Abraham's footsteps. Claim the promises and prove God. Look for the experience of the promises. You will find that the Lord is faithful. He promises that if we ask, He will do exceeding abundantly above all that we ask or think.

Standing on the promises that cannot fail,
When the howling storms of doubt and fear assail,
By the living word of God I shall prevail,
Standing on the promises of God.

CHAPTER SEVEN

IN THE PLAINS OF MAMRE - ABRAHAM'S EXAMPLE

" And the LORD appeared unto him in the plains of Mamre: and he sat in the tent door in the heat of the day; And he lift up his eyes and looked, and, lo, three men stood by him: and when he saw them, he ran to meet them from the tent door, and bowed himself toward the ground, And said, My Lord, if now I have found favour in thy sight, pass not away, I pray thee, from thy servant: Let a little water, I pray you, be fetched, and wash your feet, and rest yourselves under the tree: And I will fetch a morsel of bread, and comfort ye your hearts; after that ye shall pass on: for therefore are ye come to your servant. And they said, So do, as thou hast said. And Abraham hastened into the tent unto Sarah, and said, Make ready quickly three measures of fine meal, knead it, and make cakes upon the hearth. And Abraham ran unto the herd, and fetcht a calf tender and good, and gave it unto a

*young man; and he hasted to dress it. And he took butter,
and milk, and the calf which he had dressed, and set it
before them; and he stood by them under the tree, and
they did eat.* **//**

Genesis 18:1-8

THIS PORTION OF GENESIS RECORDS a meeting
between Abraham and some very special heavenly visitors.
The Holy Spirit has much to teach us in this passage. The first
detail we notice is that the divine name is in capital letters.
And the LORD appeared unto him in the plains of Mamre. That is
not merely a printer's device for drawing attention to the name
of our God. When the Divine name appears in capitals,
whether it be printed *LORD* or *GOD*, it signifies that, most of
the time, the incommunicable name of Jehovah is employed
in that place. We can say, therefore, that Jehovah appeared
unto Abraham in the plains of Mamre. That was a high day in
the life of Abraham.

Why then did our translators render the name *Jehovah* as
LORD? I think they learned a great deal from the Jewish
scholars and expositors, who handled the Divine name,
wherever it occurred, with the utmost reverence. Did you
know that every time a Jewish scribe put his pen to the page
to transcribe the name *Jehovah* in the Scriptures, he went away
and bathed himself from head to toe? This is incredible, but
such was their reverence for the Divine name of Jehovah.
Because the Jews, out of reverence, will not speak that name,
they say the name *Adonai* every time they come to *Jehovah* in
the text. The name *Adonai* means *Lord*, and this word, when it
appears in the text as *Lord* is spelt with an initial capital and
followed by small letters. I do believe that the translators of
the Authorized Version sought to imitate their Jewish forebears
in this matter of reverence for the name, so that Christians

would not use it lightly, especially since it occurs so many times in the Old Testament.

The nature of Abraham's audience with the Lord.

The name *Jehovah* refers to the One Who is eternal and unchanging, the same yesterday, today, and forever. He is the covenant-keeping God. We can read the verse in Genesis 18:1, *And the covenant-keeping God appeared unto him in the plains of Mamre.* We can say, the unchanging God, Who was, Who is, and Who is yet to come, met with Abraham. The unchanging God, He Who is the same yesterday, today and forever, appeared unto him while he sat in the tent door in the heat of the day. Oh that the same One Who met Abraham so many years ago would meet with us today!

And the LORD appeared unto him in the plains of Mamre: and he sat in the tent door in the heat of the day; And he lift up his eyes and looked, and, lo, three men stood by him. This seems to be a sudden meeting. Often, when the Lord begins a work, He begins it suddenly. The word *lo* means *behold.* It is the same word in the original language, whether we translate it lo or whether we translate it behold. This word should not be slighted by the reader. It indicates that God Himself calls you to give supreme attention to this portion. "Behold, look at this, pay attention to this."

Three men stood by him: and when he saw them, he ran to meet them from the tent door, and bowed himself toward the ground, And said, My Lord, if now I have found favour in thy sight, pass not away, I pray thee, from thy servant. I believe Abraham has a sense of knowing that there is something important in the air. I believe Abraham recognizes in some way his Divine visitor. *Pass not away, I pray thee.* "Lord, don't allow me now to let You go." Do you see how vitally important it is for you not only to have the sense of the Lord's presence now, but also for you to go that step further with God? There is a sense in which the Lord always abides with the Christian, that is true; but I am talking about spiritual responsibility, about seeking the presence and the blessing of the Lord. If the Lord does come near, we need to mightily lay hold on Him and say, "Lord, don't pass me by; don't leave me." If the Lord's presence is here, detain Him; hold on to Him. In God's name, don't let Him go. Would it not be grievous if others around you received a blessing from God, and you were left out?

> *Pass me not, O gentle Saviour,*
> *Hear my humble cry;*
> *While on others Thou art calling,*
> *Do not pass me by.*

The narrative of this unusual meeting goes on, *Let a little water, I pray you, be fetched, and wash your feet, and rest yourselves under the tree: And I will fetch a morsel of bread, and comfort ye your hearts; after that ye shall pass on: for therefore are ye come to your servant. And they said, So do, as thou hast said. And Abraham hastened into the tent unto Sarah, and said, Make ready quickly three measures of fine meal, knead it, and make cakes upon the hearth. And Abraham ran unto the herd, and fetcht a calf tender and good, and gave it unto a young man; and he hasted to dress it. And he took butter, and milk, and the calf which he had dressed, and set it before them; and he stood by them under the tree, and they did eat.* What a blessed time this was. What eager activity suddenly occupied this family. It seemed that Abraham could not do enough for his heavenly visitors. What an example he is to us of spiritual zeal and diligence. It seems that he could be singing, "There is Joy in Serving Jesus."

Perhaps we can see just how much Abraham exemplifies the Christian disciple and worker, the believer who is busy about the Lord's work and desirous of the Lord's pleasure, if we compare his happy activity with that of another. Genesis 19:1 says, *And there came two angels to Sodom at even; and Lot sat in the gate of Sodom: and Lot seeing them rose up to meet them; and he bowed himself with his face toward the ground; And he said, Behold now, my lords, turn in, I pray you, into your servant's house, and tarry all night, and wash your feet, and ye shall rise up early, and go on your ways. And they said, Nay; but we will abide in the street all night. And he pressed upon them greatly; and they turned in unto him and entered into his house; and he made them a feast, and did bake unleavened bread, and they did eat.*

The differences between the carnal and the spiritual man.

The reason we can learn much from the life of Abraham is because he was not only a redeemed man, but he was a spiritual man. This is a Scriptural distinction. Galatians 6:1, for example, makes this distinction: *Brethren, if a man be overtaken in a fault, ye which are spiritual, restore such an one in the spirit of meekness.*

Further, I Corinthians 3:1 not only draws this distinction, but declares that if a believer is not spiritual, he is carnal: *And I, brethren, could not speak unto you as unto spiritual, but as unto carnal, even as unto babes in Christ.* Clearly, the walk of a Christian in this life can be a spiritual walk or it can be a carnal walk.

We don't like using the word *carnal*, for we don't like to suggest, as we speak of God's people, that any of them could be such. In fact, there is a debate among a number of Christians as to whether there is such a thing as a carnal Christian. Some of these declare that a carnal Christian is really not a true Christian, that a carnal Christian is a professor who is actually unsaved. This, however, does not bear out with the plain sense of Scripture. In the first place, Paul addresses his readers in I Corinthians 3:1 as *brethren*. Now if carnal Christians are not saved, Paul has no business referring to them as brethren. But I assure you that he can. He can refer to them as brethren because they belong to the Lord, even if their lives are not showing the fruits of grace. Sadly, we have to say that the Genesis account that we have been studying has borne out the truth of this teaching as it describes the life of Lot. Lot was a carnal man, but he was saved. Scripture says he was. Another expression which we should notice in I Corinthians 3:1 is *in Christ*. The entire phrase says, *even as unto babes in Christ.* These saints of God at Corinth, even if some of them were carnal, as the Holy Ghost declared them to be, were nevertheless in Christ. Lot was in Christ, he was a spiritual brother with Abraham, but he was a carnal man. Abraham was a spiritual man.

What, then, is a spiritual man? What is a carnal man? What can we learn from thinking along this line? The Holy Spirit speaks much of the walk of the Christian, and the Lord would have us to understand that there should be a difference, a clear example, a shining testimony, in the life of a spiritual Christian. He declares, in Ephesians 2:10, *For we are his workmanship, created in Christ Jesus unto good works, which God hath before ordained that we should walk in them.* The Scripture says in Romans 6:11 and 22, *Likewise reckon ye also yourselves to be dead indeed unto sin, but alive unto God through Jesus Christ our Lord. But now being made free from sin, and become servants to God, ye have your fruit unto holiness, and the end everlasting life.* Clearly, there is a walk, a quality of life in the spiritual Christian which walks through this world with the Spirit of Christ. He looks at the world through the mind of Christ. He lives before the world for the glory of Christ. Such a person will fail and fall. He will regret that he has not lived in the light of the gospel always. He has given way to his weaknesses too often—Abraham certainly failed the Lord—but he always returns to the place of fellowship with the One at the altar. He always longs to be on redemption ground, and his walk, therefore, reflects the grace of the Saviour. He is an example of the believer in word and deed.

What is a carnal Christian? He is described in the second verse of I Corinthians 3 this way: *I have fed you with milk, and not with meat: for hitherto ye were not able to bear it, neither yet now are ye able. For ye are yet carnal: for whereas there is among you envying, and strife, and divisions, are ye not carnal, and walk as men?* Now we all "walk as men" in the sense that we are human and live in this world. But Paul here is clearly saying that the carnal Christian walks in the world much like the people of the world walk. It is difficult to see a difference between the carnal Christian and the unsaved man. What an indictment! If our Saviour gave His life to free us from the curse and power of sin, if we have been saved unto good works, if we are to be to the praise of His glory, and yet are "walking as men," we have failed God's purpose for our lives. We have betrayed the Saviour's love. We are grieving the Holy Spirit Who has regenerated and indwelt us. Three distinctive features characterize the carnal believer.

1.   **The carnal man suffers from a lack of growth.** Paul calls the carnal Christian *a babe in Christ.* This believer does not show any progress in the Christian life worth talking about. He may be called a babe in Christ because he has not grown in any perceivable way in the things of the Lord. Practically from the time he was saved, he has made very little headway. Something is wrong, for the little babe is still on the milk. If you had a sirloin steak or even a fillet steak, you would not want to give it to that tiny babe; it could do nothing with it. How many Christians in these days—and there seem to be large numbers—cannot endure strong meat? They have never shown an interest in the deep things of the Word. They live on the surface. I don't know how long now you have been on the Christian pathway. Perhaps you are a new Christian. Perhaps, on the other hand, you have been saved for thirty, forty, even fifty years, and yet have not made any perceivable progress in all that while. You are not growing in grace; you are not making advancement in the Christian life, if we are to be truthful. Now God knows your heart, and there is little use in your drawing your hypocritical garments about yourself. Hiding from the truth will never help you. Are you yet a babe in Christ? What is the answer to your lack of growth? The Scripture says we are to grow in two ways: in the *grace* and the *knowledge* of the Lord Jesus Christ. We are to know more about Him, and we are to become more *like* Him. Christ is always the answer to every need, the point of beginning and ending. Where do

we find Him? We find Him in the Scripture. We must
search for Him in the pages of Holy Writ. As we look into
His face, as we see Him in all His beauty, as we read of
His great love for us, we grow to become more like Him,
for His love constrains us. We also find Him in a spirit-
filled church that preaches Christ. Churches that preach
principles and plans miss the Person. Christ alone can
change your life. Feed upon Him. He is the Bread of Life.
He will nourish your poor soul so that it flourishes.

2.   **The carnal man exhibits divisiveness.** *For whereas there is
among you envying, and strife, and divisions, are ye not carnal?*
The apostle presses the argument home. He says that if
there is a readiness to engage in strife, if there is a readiness
to indulge in envying, and if there is a spirit of divisiveness
in your heart against other Christians, or family members,
or those with whom you associate, then there is something
very wrong. You are showing evidence of carnality. We
saw Lot as ready to engage in strife with Abraham's
herdsmen; yet we saw Abraham seek to make peace and
settle as kindly as possible with his nephew. How can you
walk in Abraham's example? You must ask for the Holy
Spirit to fill your soul with His power. You must repent of
this sin, and plead the precious blood of Christ shed for
you to cover your soul and protect it from a critical,
irritable spirit. The answer to a divisive attitude is to
remember how Christ has treated you with love and
patience, how He saved you when you were yet in your
sin, to remember His mercy when you deserved none. This
is the way to treat others.

3.   **The carnal man concentrates on worldly things.** The fact
that the carnal Christian has not grown shows us that he
does not spend time with the Saviour, or spend time in
fellowship with God's people. He fills his time with
worldly pursuits. He may not pursue activities that are
wrong in themselves or downright sinful. No, he just

spends so much time with them that there is not time for spiritual pursuits. Perhaps these activities seem so right, so harmless—hobbies, political pursuits, personal indulgences—that he does not recognize the fact that they have taken his first love. That he is quick to quarrel demonstrates that the things of the world are more important to him than walking in peace and godliness before men. His priorities are earthly, not spiritual. We saw Abraham leave country and home for Christ's sake. He staked his very life on God's promises to him. He concentrated on what God told him, and lived accordingly. Lot, on the other hand, valued comfort and prosperity. His priorities were centered in what he could gain if he moved closer to Sodom. Scripture admonishes us in Colossians 3:1, 2 *If ye then be risen with Christ, seek those things which are above, where Christ sitteth on the right hand of God. Set your affection upon things above, and not on things on the earth.* Matthew 6:19, 20 says, *Lay not up for yourselves treasures upon earth, where moth and rust doth corrupt, and where thieves break through and steal: But lay up for yourselves treasures in heaven, where neither moth nor rust doth corrupt, and where thieves do not break through nor steal: For where your treasure is, there will your heart be also.* My friend, if you know your interests reside in things which are not really helpful spiritually (even if they are legitimate things), if you are spending so much time with them that you must truthfully say that you have no time to pray and read your Bible, then you are not going on with God. We must put you in this sad category of the believer who has missed his way.

Of course, the presence of these three characteristics in the life of a Christian—spiritual immaturity, a critical, divisive spirit, and worldly priorities—means that this believer will look like the world, talk like the world, and act like the world. The carnal believer does not show much of a difference from the unbeliever to the outside observer. He might even be going to the same places that the ungodly frequent. Sadly, he may actually fall into the lifestyle of the ungodly. His speech may give no hint that he belongs to the Saviour. This man is playing with fire. Oh, my friend, have you fallen into such a condition? Flee the things of the world! Their damage can be horribly scarring and devastating. Stay away from that fire as far as you can. Otherwise, you will be the loser at the end of the day. Remember Lot. Remember Lot's wife. Follow in the footsteps of Abraham. That is the way of peace and joy.

Nine ways by which these differences are carefully highlighted in the scripture record.

Let us now turn to Genesis 18 and 19 to see the details that help us to follow Abraham's example and eschew Lot's foolishness. We will see, in the very smallest particulars of this account, how the spiritual man's walk shouts a godly testimony to the world around him.

1. **The place he occupies as he meets with a heavenly visitor—the plains of Mamre.** Abraham is found in the plains of Mamre, which is a place outside the camp. Abraham has moved as far away as he can get from Sodom. He is in the place where the Lord meets with him and blesses him. He is in a peaceful place. Lot, however, is discovered sitting in the gate of Sodom when he receives his heavenly visitors. He is in among the ungodly. No wonder Lot is unhappy; he is vexing his soul from day to day as he endures the wicked atmosphere of the city. He is still in the wrong place, out of the will of God, involved in other interests. Oh beware, child of God, of being in the wrong place. Wherever that place is, and you are the best person to recognize it, you need to get away. Listen to the still, small voice of the Lord counselling you, advising you, warning you that you should not be there. Pay heed now to the voice of the Lord.

Jesus calls us from the worship
Of the vain world's golden store,
From each idol that would keep us,
Saying, "Christian, love Me more."

2. **The line of distinction he draws—the way of the LORD.**
Abraham's life demonstrates a very different pattern from
the heathen around him. He draws away from the world,
He builds an altar to the Lord, and the Scripture says he
commands his household in *the way of the LORD*. God
Himself testifies of this spiritual man in Genesis 18:19, *For*
I know him, that he will command his children and his household
after him, and they shall keep the way of the LORD, to do justice
and judgment; that the LORD may bring upon Abraham that
which he hath spoken of him. The men of the world can see a
difference in Abraham, and they know he is not a part of
their ways. Lot, on the other hand, calls the wicked in
Sodom brethren. He is not prepared to draw the line of
distinction. Genesis 19:7 finds Lot remonstrating with the
wicked men of the city, *I pray you, brethren, do not so*
wickedly. How incredible, that in the midst of a horribly
evil situation, Lot thinks to call these perverted people
brethren. It is strange how the Christian can start watering
down the truth. Once his heart is not right, once he
wanders away from the will of God, once he starts settling
in among the ungodly, it is amazing how the child of God
can care less and less about the truth and can even call the
wicked of Sodom—those already on the precipice of
disaster, near the edge of hell, ready for the flames of
damnation—*brethren!*

3. **The One he looks to for approval—the Lord.** The
Scripture tells us in Genesis 18 that when Abraham's
heavenly visitors appear, Abraham runs to meet them,
bows down, and says, *My Lord, if now I have found favour*

in thy sight, pass not away, I pray thee, from thy servant.
Abraham desires the Lord's blessing, His smile. He takes
care to obey Him, to jump to serve Him. Indeed the Lord
is pleased with Abraham, for He says in verse 18, *all the*
nations of the earth shall be blessed in him. We know, from
the chapters preceding, that Abraham has disowned
everything belonging to Sodom. He does not want even a
thread or a shoelatchet. We can see that he cares nothing
for the devil's honours. The king of Sodom wanted to
persuade him, "Ah, give me the souls, and you take the
goods for yourself. You can have the bangles and the
bracelets and the all the valuables, the spoils which testify
to your victory." But Abraham has made it clear: "You
will not honour me. I don't need the honours of Sodom. If
I am going to seek any honour, I want the honour that
comes from on high." Poor Lot. It seems that he doesn't
know any better than to look for praise in the gate of
Sodom. He must ingratiate himself with the wicked,
calling them *brethren*, in the hope that some honour may
come his way. Oh, Lot, this is wood, hay and stubble. This
is honour that will burn in smoke and ashes soon. Have
you weighed your own life in this matter, my friend?
Where are you looking for approval? Are you looking for
the praise of men rather than the praise of God?

4.   **The dwelling he chooses—the tent.** Throughout Genesis
18, the Holy Spirit informs us that Abraham is still living
in a tent: verse 1, *and he sat in the tent door; verse 2, he ran to*
meet them from the tent door; verse 6, *And Abraham hastened*
into the tent; verse 9, *Behold, in the tent; verse 10, And Sarah*
heard it in the tent door. The patriarch is living in a tent, this
great man, the father of them that believe! You will
remember that the tent is the badge of the pilgrim.
Abraham has determined that all the while he is here, he
will stand before God as one on a journey, never, never as
one who belongs to this world. He understands that he
must hold lightly to the things of time. He is ready to pull

up the stakes, to cut the cords, when God says to move on. He is ready to follow the Lord anywhere He leads. He does not put down roots. Chapter 19 tells us that the man Lot, on the other hand, is dwelling in a house. Four times in that chapter we are reminded of where he is living. Lot, who has had great opportunity to learn from his godly uncle, has chosen to live in a permanent dwelling in Sodom. He is totally involved in that city; he is taken up with that place. He wants to belong. He has forgotten the tent. He has forgotten the Lord. How is it with you, dear friend? Are you hanging on for dear life to everything you seem to have in this world? Are you determined to keep hold of the things of time and sense? Is your view of the heavenly city so dim, that all you can see is the house on some patch of ground that you must have? Oh, there is nothing wrong with the things, the homes the Lord gives us while we occupy in this life, but have these things taken first place in our hearts? Are you ready to move at a moment's notice, to go where the Lord says to go?

Ready to go, ready to stay,
Ready my place to fill;
Ready for service lowly or great,
Ready to do His will.

5.   **The way he sees the Lord—in the light.** It would be easy to miss this detail in the beginning narration of chapter 18. *And the LORD appeared unto him in the plains of Mamre: and he sat in the tent door in the heat of the day.* The time that Abraham meets the Lord is at high noon. What is the heat of the day? That is the time when the sun has risen to its zenith in the sky. It is the time when the light is brightest, when there is not a shadow above, anywhere in the sky. Out of that bright blue sky, the sun is shining in all its fullness. If ever there were a time to meet the Lord and look into His eyes, you would want it to be when you could see His wonderful face. There wouldn't be a better

time than high noon. What a marvelous experience—the full light of Heaven's sunshine lights up the Saviour's face. Oh, that we might be in the light, so that we might behold Him in all His glory. I John 1:7, *But if we walk in the light, as he is in the light, we have fellowship one with another, and the blood of Jesus Christ his Son cleanseth us from all sin.* We know from this wonderful passage that Abraham has fellowship with the Lord. He meets with Him in the light. What a blessed time for the patriarch. Now notice the detail in Genesis 19:1, *And there came two angels to Sodom at even; and Lot sat in the gate of Sodom.* The sun is going down in Sodom. The shadows are lengthening. Darkness is coming on when Lot receives his heavenly visitors, and they are gone before the light of day. Abraham sees the Lord; Lot sees the angels. To Abraham there is not a cloud between him and the Saviour, but Lot is sitting in the shadows in the gate of Sodom. If he tries to look into the face of his heavenly visitor, it will be with difficulty. He cannot discern the features of the visitor who has come from on high. We say to Lot's everlasting discredit, the shadow he is standing in is the shadow of Sodom. What a shameful, regrettable place to be. The shadows remind us of wrongdoing, compromise, carnality, an evil departure from God. It reminds us also, that the day of grace is quickly drawing to a close. You do not want to be in that shadow. One interesting word study may help you to see how God views Lot. In Isaiah 25:7, you will find the Hebrew word translated *covering* in the text: *And he will destroy in this mountain the face of the covering cast over all people, and the vail that is spread over all nations.* This prophecy speaks of the time when the Lord returns and ransoms the redeemed of Israel. The elect remnant in the tribes of Israel will look unto Him and find Him as their Saviour and Redeemer. The word, *mountain*, refers to Israel, the land of hills and valleys. This verse tells us that the joyful day will come when God's ancient people will be brought out of their blindness and will be blessed of

God. The covering over their eyes will be removed and they will see their King in His glory. The Hebrew word for *covering* is the same word as *Lot*. His name in Hebrew means *covering*. When you think of Lot, think of the man who is standing in the shadows. His eyes cannot see clearly spiritual things. He has a covering across his face, a kind of veil that makes the things of the Lord dark. There is the celestial visitor, true enough, but he cannot see him clearly, and he cannot perceive the sense of his message. Are we not preaching oftentimes to some of God's people who cannot see the issue? They go back into the world week after week into the same old ways. They just cannot see clearly. God will have to lift the veil and take it away from their eyes. That is mainly what revival is about—God anointing the eyes of His people and showing them the difference between the things of this world, and the things of eternity, impressing them with the reality of things to come. That is revival; that is God working. Are God's people blinded with the veil, blighted with the character of Sodom and Egypt? Let us pray for revival, that we may walk in the light and have fellowship with our Saviour, as did Abraham.

Walk in the light! So shalt thou know
That fellowship of love
His Spirit only can bestow
Who reigns in light above.

Walk in the light! And thou shalt find
Thy heart made truly His,
Who dwells in cloudless light enshrined,
In Whom no darkness is.

Walk in the light! Thy path shall be
A path, though thorny, bright;
For God, by grace, shall dwell in thee,
And God Himself is light.

6. **The quality of his fellowship with the Lord—perfect accord.** Genesis 18 tells us that when the Lord comes to Abraham, the man of God says, "Now let me prepare something to refresh you, body and soul. Let me bring a vessel of water and I will wash your feet. Let me prepare some food for you before you must pass on." The response of the heavenly visitors to Abraham's offer is, *So do, as thou hast said.* The Bible tells us that Abraham prepares bountifully for his guests. This great man, eminent as he is, kneels down to wash the feet of these visitors. He thinks nothing of humbling himself in the dust. Abraham wishes to share his hospitality and his table with the Lord, and the Lord encourages Abraham, "Go ahead and do that. I would be glad to sit at your table." That is beautiful! What a special time they must have under the tree as the Lord receives Abraham's hospitality and fellowship. What pleasant conversation they must share during that noonday meal.

'Tis the blessed hour of prayer, when our hearts lowly bend,
And we gather to Jesus, our Saviour and Friend;
If we come to Him in faith, His protection to share,
What a balm for the weary! O how sweet to be there!

At the blessed hour of prayer, trusting Him we believe
That the blessings we're needing we'll surely receive;
In the fullness of this trust we shall lose every care;
What a balm for the weary! O how sweet to be there!

But let us look at the scene in Genesis 19. Lot is receiving his visitors with typical eastern hospitality. He says, "Come into the house, stay the night, wash your feet." Notice how Lot, really a nobody in the town of Sodom, says, "Wash your own feet." And what do the guests say? Genesis 19:2, *Nay; but we will abide in the street all night.* What is this? The heavenly visitors have come especially on Lot's account. They have no other business there than to tell Lot to get out. They have come to see this man, yet they are loath to cross his threshold. Wicked as Sodom is, these celestial guests prefer to sit on Lot's doorstep and spend the night in the street rather than enter into his dwelling. Oh, there must be something wrong in that home, when the Lord does not want to enter. Lot is a saved man. This is a Christian home, believe it or not, in Sodom; yet the angel of God would not want to be in it, preferring to remain in the streets of that wicked city. Lot's home must not be a happy place if the Lord is absent. I think the devil runs wild in that home. Abraham lives in a tent, but the Lord comes and has sweet fellowship. I would rather live in a tent with the Lord's presence than dwell in a mansion without Him.

Happy the home when God is there,
And love fills every breast;
When one their wish, and one their prayer,
And one their heav'nly rest.

Happy the home where Jesus' Name
Is sweet to every ear;
Where children early lisp His fame,
And parents hold Him dear.

Happy the home where prayer is heard,
And praise is wont to rise;
Where parents love the sacred Word,
And all its wisdom prize.

Lord, let us in our homes agree
This blessed peace to gain;
Unite our hearts in love to Thee,
And love to all will reign.

7. **The nature of his giving—generous.** Have you ever noticed the modesty of those who serve the Lord

sacrificially? Often those who do the most to further His kingdom, do it with quietness and self-deprecation, as if it were very little to offer Him. They do tremendous things and will not let it be noticed. Their attitude is, "I am at best an unprofitable servant." Indeed, the more we realize what the Lord has done for us, the more we see that the little we do for Him is small indeed. Abraham reflects this attitude by the manner in which he receives his heavenly guests. In Genesis 18: 4 and 5, he seems to offer just a small bit of hospitality: *Let a little water, I pray you, be fetched. . .And I will fetch a morsel of bread.* Let us go through the account and find out just what is this wee morsel. We read in Genesis 18:6-8, *And Abraham hastened into the tent unto Sarah, and said, Make ready quickly three measures of fine meal, knead it, and make cakes upon the hearth. And Abraham ran unto the herd, and fetcht a calf tender and good, and gave it unto a young man; and he hasted to dress it. And he took butter, and milk, and the calf which he had dressed, and set it before them.* That is quite a morsel! There is tender beef, freshly dressed and roasted, milk, and cakes made from newly ground meal, just hot from the oven and slathered with butter. It is a sumptuous feast, fit for a king, and Abraham makes nothing of it. He calls it just a morsel. Abraham gives the best that he has to the Lord. He sees it as the least that he can do. Does this not speak to us concerning our work for the Saviour? Does not the spiritual man have such a sense of the Lord's goodness to him that he finds joy in doing all he can for the One Who has given His life for his salvation? Of course, there are other people who really do very little in the work, and they talk about that very little to the band playing as if it were just the greatest thing. Chapter 19, verse 3 says, *and he made them a feast, and did bake unleavened bread, and they did eat.* The feast that Lot provides consists of unleavened bread. Let me change the terminology. Maybe the nearest thing to unleavened bread that you have ever known would be cream crackers. Imagine a sturdy man who can build up a great appetite.

He comes home in the evening time and expects his wife to have prepared something fairly substantial. Imagine his wife saying, "You have worked hard all day, dear. I tell you, I have a real feast for you tonight." Her husband's eyes light up with expectancy. She turns around and brings from the cupboard a plate with two or three cream crackers—no butter—just cream crackers. This is the feast she has prepared! This is exactly what Lot has done. He has the audacity to speak about making a feast, and offers a few cream crackers. He makes a great deal of it even though it is nothing.

I gave My life for thee,
My precious blood I shed,
That thou might'st ransomed be,
And quickened from the dead;
I gave, I gave My life for thee,
What hast thou given for Me?

And I have brought to thee,
Down from My home above,
Salvation full and free,
My pardon and My love;
I bring, I bring rich gifts to thee,
What hast thou brought to Me?

8. **The spirit of his response—zealous.** Once again, let us view the scene in the plain of Mamre. Abraham is sitting in the door of his tent in the heat of the day. Now the midday sun in the Middle East can be paralyzing because of its intensity. Abraham is resting in the middle of the day perhaps because of the heat, or perhaps because he has been working hard, and has sat down to rest or reflect. Perhaps he is in prayer. He looks up to see three men standing before him. You would think that in such heat, he would take a bit of time to get up. He might even remain in the shade of the tent door and let the visitors come to

him. This would to be a reasonable response, especially since Abraham is an old man now. Verse 11 says, *Now Abraham and Sarah were old and well stricken in age.* But this spiritual man senses the Lord's presence. He walks in fellowship with the Lord, and he knows this is a special moment. He does not want the Lord to pass him by. He won't miss this momentous meeting. Genesis 18:2, 6, 7: *And when he saw them, he ran to meet them from the tent door. . .And Abraham hastened into the tent unto Sarah, and said, Make ready quickly three measures of fine meal. . .And Abraham ran unto the herd, and fetcht a calf tender and good, and gave it unto a young man; and he hasted to dress it.* This description does not fit the picture of an old man who is paralyzed by the midday heat. Oh, when you do work for God, put your heart and soul into it. This is how the patriarch Abraham responds to his celestial visitors. We see no such response in Lot. Genesis 19:16 says, *And while he lingered, the men laid hold upon his hand.* Verse 15 tells us that *the angels hastened Lot.* They actually find it necessary to take him by the hand and lead him out! The Scripture record here forever impresses upon our minds the response of the carnal man to the urging of God upon his heart: he lingers. He must be pushed, hurried. These heavenly visitors are rushing. They feel the urgency of God's judgement. This city is sliding down over the edge into hell. They have cried out their warning, and Lot is lingering. He is hanging back, unwilling to obey and maybe even resentful. Abraham runs; Lot lingers. Abraham hastens; the angels hasten Lot. Abraham is not in danger like Lot, but yet he runs. On the other hand, Lot is in unspeakable and imminent danger this night, but he lingers. What is wrong with you? All the while God is working. All the while God is speaking. Instead of running with joy and running with eagerness to do what the Lord asks, you are hanging back and lingering. My Christian friend, are you slow to do the right thing? Some of you exhibit great diligence in everyday affairs, and there is nothing wrong with this; but when the Spirit of God urges you about some matter in your own soul, you find you are not as diligent. Abraham ran. No wonder God blessed him. I tell you, no wonder God blessed the man. These things matter.

My heart, how dreadful hard it is!
How heavy here it lies!
Heavy and cold within my breast,
Just like a rock of ice!

Sin, like a raging tyrant, sits
Upon this flinty throne,
And ev'ry grace lies buried deep
Beneath this heart of stone.

How seldom do I rise to God,
Or taste the joys above!
This mountain presses down my faith,
And chills my flaming love.

When smiling mercy courts my soul
With all its heav'nly charms,
This stubborn, this relentless thing
Would thrust it from my arms.

Against the thunders of thy word
Rebellious I have stood;
My heart, it shakes not at the wrath
And terrors of a God.

Dear Saviour, steep this rock of mine
In thine own crimson sea!
None but a bath of blood divine
Can melt the flint away.

9. **The reward for his obedience—the Lord Himself.** Back
    in Genesis 15:1, we saw the words, *After these things the
    word of the LORD came unto Abram in a vision, saying, Fear
    not, Abram: I am thy shield, and thy exceeding great reward.*
    Then the Lord speaks to him again in chapter 17:1, when
    Abraham is ninety-nine years of age. I love that. I am glad
    that I find such a word in the Bible. Even though this man
    would be on the borders of making the century, the Lord
    has not forgotten about him. The Lord is still speaking to
    him. He still has his senses. He can still figure out the
    things of God. The old mind seems to be as clear as a bell.
    You can ask the Lord to give you a keen mind in old age,
    but if you are not using your mind to glorify Him, if you
    are not thinking upon His Person and His Gospel, you
    have hardly the right to ask the Lord for a clear mind. If
    you have no thoughts for Him, no wonder the mind might
    go. God says to this patriarch of ninety-nine years, *I am
    the Almighty God; walk before me, and be thou perfect.* These
    are God's words to your own soul just as sure as ever
    anything has ever come to that soul of yours. I am the
    Almighty God. He is still the same God today. Abraham's
    God still lives today. *I am the Almighty God; walk before me.*
    Listen, God is speaking to you. He is speaking to you so
    clearly I may as well call your name. It could not be plainer.
    Abraham, the spiritual believer, has wanted nothing out
    of Sodom. He wants a heavenly reward. He knows the
    difference. He looks for a city whose builder and maker is
    God. He longs to hear the "well done" of the Saviour. He
    expects the fulfillment of the covenant promises. He
    knows that he has obtained an inheritance in Christ Jesus,
    for he has seen His day, and is glad. Abraham has turned
    his back on the paltry trinkets and the influence of Sodom,
    for he is a spiritual man, a man who walks in the Spirit of
    Christ. Lot, on the other hand, has been dim of vision. He
    has had eyes only for this world. He has invested all of
    twenty years' labour and effort in Sodom, only to see it
    all go up in smoke. I Corinthians 3:13 tells us that *the fire*

shall try every man's work of what sort it is. So it will. When the fire comes down on Sodom, all of Lot's work will go up in smoke and ashes. There will be nothing left for it is just stubble. I John 2:28 instructs us, *And now, little children, abide in him; that, when he shall appear, we may have confidence, and not be ashamed before him at his coming.* There are some of us who have walked a carnal pathway. We have not grown nor spent our years seeking after the things of God. We have sown bitterness and discontent everywhere we have gone. Some of us are going to be ashamed—oh, so ashamed—at the Lord's coming. The question that I am leaving with you is, "How are you going to meet the Lord in that great day?" Perhaps you have recognized yourself as a carnal Christian. God can restore the years the locusts have eaten. Just as we have been redeemed through the Lord Jesus, so we can be cleansed from our carnal ways through His blood. The invitation in Revelation 3:20 is still open: *Behold, I stand at the door, and knock; if any man hear my voice, and open the door, I will come in to him, and will sup with him, and he with me.*

O Jesus, Thou art standing
Outside the fast-closed door,
In lowly patience waiting
To pass the threshold o'er.
Shame on us, Christian brothers,
His name and sign who bear,
Oh, shame, thrice shame upon us,
To keep Him standing there!

O Jesus, Thou art knocking:
And lo, that hand is scarred,
And thorns Thy brow encircle,
And tears thy face have marred.
O love that passeth knowledge,
So patiently to wait!
O sin that hath no equal,
So fast to bar the gate!

O Jesus, Thou art pleading
In accents meek and low,
"I died for you, my children,
And will ye treat Me so?"
O Lord, with shame and sorrow
We open now the door;
Dear Saviour, enter, enter,
And leave us nevermore.

Oh, that everyone of us might be able to say, "Lord, Thou hast spoken. I have heard Thy voice, and it has been a word in season. Thou hast suffered and died on the tree, and finished that grand work of redemption for me. Help me along the road to glory. Allow me to be a witness for Thee. Allow me to have the heavenly vision as Abraham did." *Beloved, now are we the sons of God, and it doth not yet appear what we shall be: but we know that, when he shall appear, we shall be like him; for we shall see him as he is.* What a reward! What a Saviour!

CHAPTER EIGHT

INTO THE LAND OF MORIAH-
ABRAHAM'S SACRIFICE

" *And it came to pass after these things, that God did tempt Abraham, and said unto him, Abraham: and he said, Behold, here I am. And he said, Take now thy son, thine only son Isaac, whom thou lovest, and get thee into the land of Moriah; and offer him there for a burnt offering upon one of the mountains which I will tell thee of. And Abraham rose up early in the morning, and saddled his ass, and took two of his young men with him, and Isaac his son, and clave the wood for the burnt offering, and rose up, and went unto the place of which God had told him. Then on the third day Abraham lifted up his eyes, and saw the place afar off. And Abraham said unto his young men, Abide ye here with the ass; and I and the lad will go yonder and worship, and come again to you. And Abraham took the wood of the burnt offering, and laid it upon Isaac his son; and he took the fire in his hand, and a knife; and they went both of them*

together. And Isaac spake unto Abraham his father, and said, My father: and he said, Here am I, my son. And he said, Behold the fire and the wood: but where is the lamb for a burnt offering? And Abraham said, My son, God will provide himself a lamb for a burnt offering: so they went both of them together. And they came to the place which God had told him of; and Abraham built an altar there, and laid the wood in order, and bound Isaac his son, and laid him on the altar upon the wood. And Abraham stretched forth his hand, and took the knife to slay his son. And the angel of the LORD called unto him out of heaven, and said, Abraham, Abraham: and he said, Here am I. And he said, Lay not thine hand upon the lad, neither do thou any thing unto him: for now I know that thou fearest God, seeing thou hast not withheld thy son, thine only son from me. And Abraham lifted up his eyes, and looked, and behold behind him a ram caught in a thicket by his horns: and Abraham went and took the ram, and offered him up for a burnt offering in the stead of his son. And Abraham called the name of that place Jehovah-jireh: as it is said to this day, In the mount of the LORD it shall be seen. And the angel of the LORD called unto Abraham out of heaven the second time, And said, By myself have I sworn, saith the LORD, for because thou hast done this thing, and hast not withheld thy son, thine only son: That in blessing I will bless thee, and in multiplying I will multiply thy seed as the stars of the heaven, and as the sand which is upon the sea shore; and thy seed shall possess the gate of his enemies; And in thy seed shall all the nations of the earth be blessed; because thou hast obeyed my voice. So Abraham returned unto his young men, and they rose up and went together to Beer-sheba; and Abraham dwelt at Beer-sheba. **"**

Genesis 22:1-19

YEARS HAVE PASSED. ABRAHAM HAS experienced terrible disappointment, and indescribable joy. He has prevailed in intercessory prayer, demonstrated loyalty and courage in battle, and walked with God. He has learned that the covenant promises will not be realized in Ishmael, the child of the flesh and the son of the bondwoman. He has lived to see the birth of Isaac, the child of the covenant, the son of his old age, and the offspring of Sarah who was past the age to bear children.

We have followed this man, the father of the faithful, the resolute disciple of Christ, the friend of God; surely we have seen everything in a consecrated life that we could ever hope to observe. But no. We follow him now to the high point of his walk with God, the pinnacle of his faith, the climax of long years spent following and honouring the Lord. Here, in Genesis 22, is so profound an example of his love, his obedience, and his devotion to God, that we are privileged to see the crowning act of discipleship in the life of this venerable patriarch. And in viewing the scene in this chapter, we come to the incredible conclusion that Abraham has never really found out what it means to leave all for his Saviour, to put God first, until he climbs that rugged hill of Moriah.

Genesis 22, verse 1, describes the strangest of all experiences to Abraham: *And it came to pass after these things, that God did tempt Abraham.* In this place, the word *tempt* means to *test*. Now God is testing Abraham, testing his discipleship. To put it simply, Abraham cannot reach the pinnacle of faith without God's proving him. He cannot be considered the resolute disciple of the Lord without his reaching a point of crisis at the altar. Genesis 22 makes it clear that before this man, this highly honoured servant of God reaches the end of his days, he will not only test God, but the Lord will test *him*. Abraham is surely one of the Lord's most beloved servants, and now he must submit to testing. We are not left to imagine that Abraham is some sort of "fair weather" follower of the Lord, but in this instance, as no other man, Abraham's **faith** is tested, his **love** is tested, his **will to obey God** is put to the test. And we may follow in his steps—though we're not fit to lace his shoes—I say, we may follow in his steps because every child of God must come to the point of testing.

So then, Genesis 22 teaches us that **the Lord must test every one of His servants.** Nobody will be an exception. The Lord will test even the best of His people. The child of God must never imagine that he can set out to prove God, without the Lord's proving him! Nobody can get by then without a time of testing, and I must say to you, that you should *expect* a time of testing in your Christian walk.

Strangely today, in the world of the charismatic Christian, it is thought that there is no such thing as being put to the test under God's hand, that there is no affliction in the life of a victorious believer. Charismatism declares the promise of victory, but in reality, it is an empty, false victory. The constant emphasis on experiencing victory blots out the possibility of affliction in its followers' minds, yet God does test every one of His people. Victory is not won without a battle. These people will come to the time when their love is put to the test, when their faith passes through the crucible, when their obedience is weighed in the balance. And when these people reach that time of crisis, their theories of easy victory will provide no answer for their situation. Darkness will fill their hearts.

Many a child of God has backslidden. And when you probe into the matter, you find that he has had a time of testing, and it has left him without an answer. My friend, you have to know that the Lord must test your profession; He must test your stand. He must prove your love for Him, love for His Book, love for His people and love for His day. *Beloved, think it not strange concerning the fiery trial which is to try you, as though some strange thing happened unto you: But rejoice, inasmuch as ye are partakers of Christ's sufferings; that, when his glory shall be revealed, ye may be glad also with exceeding joy* (II Peter 4:12,13).

Not only will God prove every one of His servants, but when the Lord begins to test you, **He always puts your name**

on the message as He speaks. There it is in verse 1: *And it came to pass after these things, that God did tempt Abraham, and said unto him, Abraham.* Maybe the Lord has been speaking to you.

When there is a time of testing, it just seems that the Lord separates you from the rest of His people. And for a fact, the Lord puts your name on the message. The test is yours, but you are not alone. The Lord may bring you apart for a time, but nothing can separate you from the love of God, which is in Christ Jesus. You are His child. Listen for your name, for His voice.

Speak to me by name, O Master,
Let me know it is to me;
Speak, that I may follow faster,
With a step more firm and free,
Where the Shepherd leads the flock,
In the shadow of the Rock.

Master, speak! and make me ready,
When Thy voice is truly heard,
With obedience glad and steady
Still to follow ev'ry word.
I am list'ning, Lord, for Thee;
Master, speak, oh, speak to me!

Every one should observe the prompt and ready response of Abraham, when he entered into severest trial.

Listen to how Abraham responds to God's voice. What remarkable words these are! *Behold, here I am.* And his response does not change over time. There is no indication in the chapter after this initial response, that Abraham ever hesitates, or that he ever questions the Lord. I don't see one thing in the verses that follow, as God reveals the requirements of this test, to suggest that Abraham thinks he has spoken too soon or too hurriedly. No, I can see that readiness, that wholehearted and immediate submission to the will of God in everything that follows in the chapter. **To be a disciple of Christ, you must leave all for Him. To be a disciple of Christ, you must put the Lord first. To be a disciple of Christ, you must make a wholehearted and immediate submission of your will to God.**

Abraham has declared himself ready to hear God's command—*Behold, here I am*—and what an instruction he receives! The next verse reads, *Take now thy son, thine only son Isaac, whom thou lovest, and get thee into the land of Moriah; and offer him there for a burnt offering upon one of the mountains which I will tell thee of.* Would the heart of this great man have stopped for an instant at such a poignant announcement? The Scripture does not record Abraham's emotion, but it does give us some insight when we look carefully at its spare wording. *Take now thy son, thine only son Isaac, whom thou lovest.* If you look at Genesis 22:2, you will notice that the second time the word son appears here, it is in italics. The original actually reads, *Take now thy son,* **thine only Isaac.** Certainly, God shows here that He knows how much Abraham loves his son. He is acknowledging that indeed, Isaac is the promised heir, the son of his old age, the child of the covenant, the channel of the blessing God has promised to Abraham. He is greatly beloved, for he is his only son. HeH The sense of this passage would read, "Take now thy son, the darling of thy bosom, thine only Isaac, the son thou dost love so much." And we could also say that the wording is such that God is instructing His servant, "Take now thy son, the darling of thy bosom, thine only Isaac, and **nobody else but Isaac.**"

And what would God have Abraham do with his beloved son? *Get thee into the land of Moriah; and offer him there for a burnt offering upon one of the mountains which I will tell thee of.* Look closely at this heart-piercing directive. The first order, *Get thee into the land of Moriah,* would mean, "Go alone to that hill, the hill of Moriah. Go to that place of sacrifice. " The words seem to suggest that Abraham must do this on his own. There is no record of Abraham's discussing the issue with Sarah. I don't know what would have ensued if he had said, "I am taking Isaac today and using this knife on him. I am going to slay him." I do not know whether his dear wife would have got in his way. But Abraham understands these words to be for him. He is keeping his own counsel.

God's dealings with Abraham uniformly conform to the pattern set in chapter twelve.

The language of this simple command in the original is very much like the language we saw in Genesis 12:1: *Get thee out of thy country, and from thy kindred, and from thy father's house.* Remember, that the sense of this passage was, "Go, for your own sake, out of this country, forsaking your friends." It was part one of God's commandments, and now, this order in Genesis 22 is part two, and the final part, and the greatest part of God's command unto him. *Get thee into the land of Moriah.* We see also that the blessing pronounced upon Abraham later in chapter 22 is very similar to the blessing he was promised in chapter 12. Genesis 12 declares, *And I will make of thee a great nation, and I will bless thee, and make thy name great; and thou shalt be a blessing, And I will bless them that bless thee, and curse him that curseth thee: and in thee shall all families of the earth be blessed.* God reiterates His promise here in Genesis 22:17, 18, saying, *That in blessing I will bless thee, and in multiplying I will multiply thy seed as the stars of the heaven, and as the sand which is upon the sea shore; and thy seed shall possess the gate of his enemies; And in thy seed shall all the nations of the earth be blessed; because thou hast obeyed my voice.* The circle is complete; when we arrive at this testing time in Abraham's pilgrimage, we indeed come to the pinnacle of the man's faith. This moment is the climax of long pressing on with God.

You remember that when God first called Abraham to leave his own country, He did not reveal to him his destination, but declared only, *Get thee out of thy country. . .unto a land that I will shew thee.* Hebrews 11 explains, *and he went out, not knowing whither he went.* We observe here in Genesis 22 that God's guidance in Abraham's pilgrimage continues to be gradual and progressive. He requires that Abraham proceed a step at a time. Once again the language in Genesis 22 resembles that of Genesis 12: *Get thee into the land of Moriah. . .upon one of the mountains which I will tell thee of.* It seems that this lesson is one of the most difficult that we have to learn. The Christian, in a time of testing, with a heart of unbelief, wants to see the whole story all at once. If God is leading him down some difficult path, he wants to see the end from the beginning. My friend, it's at that time you must trust. That is the time when you must take the Lord just at His Word, day by day, one day at a time. Don't be seeking to trust God for tomorrow or next week or next year, asking Him to reveal all that is ahead, or to supply a need far in advance. Just trust Him today. **Trust the Lord to get you through this day only.** Child of God in dire straits, unable to cope with your situation—I must ask you—can you trust God today? Don't worry about tomorrow. Just trust Him for what you see today, and for what you need today. The Lord says to Abraham, "Go to the land of Moriah, and I'll show you exactly where you must go and what you need to know when you get there." Abraham knows only that it is the land of Moriah to which he goes.

The day dawns. We observe this man's disciplined, submissive, trusting response to the dreaded assignment: *And Abraham rose up early in the morning, and saddled his ass, and took two of his young men with him, and Isaac his son, and clave the wood for the burnt offering, and rose up, and went unto the place of which God had told him.* I have to marvel at this. He rises early in the morning! There is no tardiness with Abraham. There is no struggle in his heart as to whether he will carry out the command, as no doubt, there would be with us. We would look for another way. We would pray again and seek from God some other message. But Abraham questions nothing! That's what I like about Abraham—he never questions that which has come to him from God. He rises early to start with

God, he saddles his beast of burden, he takes two of his young servants and Isaac his son, he prepares the wood for the burnt offering, and heads out for the place.

Four references to that sacred place God had in His heart from the beginning of time - indeed from all eternity.

And what is *the place*? Four times in this chapter the Holy Spirit uses these two words to refer to the location of the greatest test, and the greatest revelation, that Abraham will ever have.

1.   Verse 3 tells us that it is the place of which *God had told him*. It is the place described **by God**. It is the place that Abraham has heard of, by faith, from God. That is what I want you to notice about the place: it is the place that has been spoken of **by God**. It is the place selected **by God**.

2.   *Then on the third day Abraham lifted up his eyes, and saw the place afar off* (Genesis 22:4). This is Abraham's first sight of the place of which God has told him. He must feel such heaviness in his breast that he cannot breathe. How can we understand this moment for Abraham? He has set out for the distant land of Moriah. He has ascended from the south, and now this old man stands on the brow of a hill with his beloved son beside him. He looks up further northwards, and sees the hill of the skull. The Book tells us that he sees the place afar off. He knows it is the place. How does he know? He has never been here before, but he knows the place. He is told **by God**. The voice says, "This is it. You've come now."
Abraham has come to this place to lay his son on the altar. We are beginning to understand the significance of Genesis chapter 22. This chapter is all about a father who is required to give up his only son. It is about a loving father who must sacrifice his dearly beloved son, even in one sense, his only begotten son. We see John chapter 3, verse

16 in the background of this story: *For God so loved the world, that he gave his only begotten son, that whosoever believeth in him should not perish, but have everlasting life.* When this test is over for Abraham, he will understand that Moriah is the picture of that greater sacrifice. He will behold Calvary, long years ahead of time. He will see, with faith's eye, the giving of God's only begotten Son. And he will have a small realization of the great love of God, Who chose to sacrifice His Son for the sins of His people.

The love of God is greater far
Than tongue or pen can ever tell;
It goes beyond the highest star,
And reaches to the lowest hell.
The guilty pair, bowed down with care,
God gave His Son to win;
His erring child He reconciled,
And pardoned from his sin.

3. Abraham has seen the place afar off. Later in verse 9 we are told, *they came to the place.* Can we see the same experience in every disciple of the Lord? Cannot every child of God testify as to his experience in getting to the Cross? First of all, you **heard** of the place, the place called Calvary, Golgotha, the hill of the skull. And how did you hear of it? Why, you were told it **by God**! You learned of it from the Word of God. You heard it preached by a man of God. You received the knowledge of it from godly parents, a concerned Christian friend, or from caring Sabbath school teachers. In those early days you saw the place afar off. Then, in the course of time, God revealed the wonderful truth of the Cross to your soul. He spoke to you one day, and like Abraham, you rose up, and led by God's Word to your own soul, you sought the place of the skull until you came to that hill.

Years I spent in vanity and pride,
Caring not my Lord was crucified,
Knowing not it was for me He died
On Calvary.

By God's Word at last my sin I learned;
Then I trembled at the law I'd spurned,
Till my guilty soul imploring turned
To Calvary.

Mercy there was great, and grace was free;
Pardon there was multiplied to me;
There my burdened soul found liberty,
At Calvary.

Abraham and Isaac, and the young men who have come
with them, are standing a distance from the place.
Abraham turns to his servants and says, "You stay here."
He and Isaac will go on the last leg of the journey by
themselves. And the men fade out of the picture. Isn't it
true, that those who walked with Jesus for all those years
of discipleship, just faded away in the darkness of the
night, as He came to the place of the Cross? They forsook
Him and fled. They could not ascend that hill with Him.
The Saviour went on alone with His Father. The work of
the Cross was God's work alone. And although Isaac never
was forsaken by Abraham, we know that at that supreme
sacrifice, Jesus had to cry, "My God, why hast thou
forsaken me?"

It was alone the Saviour stood
In Pilate's judgment hall;
Alone the crown of thorns He wore,
Forsaken thus by all.

Alone upon the cross He hung
That others He might save;
Forsaken then by God and man,
Alone, His life He gave.

It is at this moment that we come to the words of Abraham which comprise an amazing statement of faith. Genesis 22, verse 5: A*nd Abraham said unto his young men, Abide ye here with the ass; and I and the lad will go yonder and worship, and come again to you.* Abraham is saying, "The boy and I will worship up there on that hill, and then we will return." What a declaration of utter trust and confidence! But wait. Doesn't Abraham know why he has come to Moriah? Doesn't he understand the command that God has explicitly given to him? He's to sacrifice Isaac. Isaac must be put to the sword. Remember, Abraham has waited for the birth of Isaac for many years. He prayed long before Isaac was ever born, and he knew that Isaac would bear the promised line to the Redeemer. This means that now, if he takes the knife and uses its blade on Isaac, the direct line to the Mediator will be severed! If there is no Isaac, there will be no Saviour! No Messiah! No Redeemer! Abraham knows the covenant promise. He understands all of this. We hear Abraham say to the young men, "We'll be back in a short time." *I and the lad will go. . . and worship, and come again to you.* The statement is clear. What does it mean?

Casual, unbelieving, unsympathetic readers would probably say, "Abraham was fantasizing here." I can say with a certainty that he is not. All of this is explained in the New Testament in the book of Hebrews, chapter 11, verses 17 to 19: *By faith Abraham, when he was tried, offered up Isaac: and he that had received the promises offered up his only begotten son, Of whom it was said, That in Isaac shall thy seed be called: Accounting that God was able to raise him up, even from the dead.* If we follow the statement here, the New Testament is confirming the fact that Abraham has received great promises of blessing. He has been promised a son through whom the single line to the Redeemer is to come, *for in Isaac shall thy seed be called.* He knows that to take the knife and use it on Isaac will be to cut off the line to the Redeemer. Clearly, Abraham has the thing settled in his mind. He recognizes that he must go through with God's command. And he will use the knife. He will offer him up, as God is requiring of him. But since God has promised that Isaac will continue the line to the Redeemer, it is necessary for Isaac to live. Isaac is yet called a lad. He has not married. There are no descendants from him. Therefore, Isaac cannot be cut off. Abraham has already worked this out. The Scripture says that he has taken into account that God is able to raise Isaac up. In his mind, he's thinking, "So that's it. God intends to raise him from the dead!" I admire Abraham, with his unstaggering, implicit faith in the actual Word, the literal Word of God. He believes every word that God has spoken. He believes that God is able to raise up his son.

It is now time for Abraham and his son to turn their steps towards the hill of the skull. Verse 6 describes the scene: *And Abraham took the wood of the burnt offering, and laid it upon Isaac his son; and he took the fire in his hand, and a knife; and they went both of them together.* Abraham has laid the burden of the sacrifice on his son, and Abraham bears the fire and the knife. Can we see that greater sacrifice? Did not God the Father lay upon His Son the burden of our redemption? Did not our Lord Jesus bear the weight of our sin? *Surely he hath borne our griefs, and carried our sorrows.* And did not the sharp blade of God's righteous anger flash against the Lord Jesus? Was not the fiery wrath of a holy God against the sin of His people poured out upon our Saviour? *But he was wounded for our transgressions, he was bruised for our iniquities. . .it pleased the LORD to bruise him.*

Father and son are walking together up the hill. Isaac does not yet know what God asked of Abraham. The Scripture records their conversation in the last few moments before they reach the top of the summit. Genesis 22, verses 7 and 8: *And Isaac spake unto Abraham his father, and said, My father: and he said, Here am I, my son. And he said, Behold the fire and the wood: but where is the lamb for a burnt offering? And Abraham said, My son, God will provide himself a lamb for a burnt offering: so they went both of them together.* How Abraham's heart must burn! His son trusts him. God tests him. And he utters a second, profound statement of supreme faith, My son, God will provide himself a lamb for a burnt offering. We do not overstate this moment if we say that Abraham knows that a sacrificial lamb will be provided, and that it will be **provided by God**. And the Holy Spirit records for us, in a foreshadowing of Calvary, *God will provide **himself** a lamb.*

Lamb of God! Thy Father's bosom
Ever was Thy dwelling place;
His delight, in Him rejoicing,
One with Him in pow'r and grace;
Oh, what wondrous love and mercy!
Thou did'st lay Thy glory by;
And for us did'st come from heaven
As the Lamb of God to die.

The story comes to its climax. Genesis 22:9, *And they came to the place which God had told him of; and Abraham built an altar there, and laid the wood in order.* The moment has come. Abraham cannot delay. He turns to his son, and as he has done so often before, he takes him in his arms. But this time, he embraces him with anguished soul. Scripture does not record for us the words exchanged between father and son. We know only that Isaac submits to this strange treatment, for the account reads that Abraham *bound Isaac his son, and laid him on the altar upon the wood.* What a test this is! This great man has come through many lessons in discipleship. Abraham has said goodbye to his father, who is a picture of the flesh that holds him back. He has parted from Lot, the backslider and the hindrance. He has even said goodbye to Ishmael, the son of his own efforts, and a type of the sinner and the world, which do the devil's work. Abraham, in one situation after another, has said goodbye to these and put God first every time. But these trials are nothing as compared to the one that occurs here, because Isaac is a gift from God. Isaac is his dear son. Isaac is the son of the promise, and the child of many prayers. It is the most difficult thing in the world for him to surrender to God the object of his love. He must not only give up the Lots and the Ishmaels, but he must give up Isaac, to put the Saviour first.

Events move quickly now. *And Abraham stretched forth his hand, and took the knife to slay his son.* Abraham raises the knife over the body of Isaac. He must obey. He prepares to plunge the knife into the breast of his dear son—and God intervenes. *And the angel of the LORD called unto him out of heaven, and said, Abraham, Abraham: and he said, Here am I. And he said, Lay not thine hand upon the lad, neither do thou any thing unto him; for now I know that thou fearest God, seeing thou hast not withheld thy son, thine only son from me.* Abraham has passed the test. His discipleship, his love for God, his obedience have been weighed, and they have not been found wanting. *God is faithful, who will not suffer you to be tempted above that ye are able; but will with the temptation also make a way to escape.*

There is more to come. God is not finished. Genesis 22:13 reads, *And Abraham lifted up his eyes, and looked, and behold behind him a ram caught in a thicket by his horns; and Abraham went and took the ram, and offered him up for a burnt offering in the stead of his son.* Relieved, Abraham turns around, where an incredible sight meets his eyes. A ram is tangled in a bush nearby, so that he cannot escape! Indeed, God has provided a lamb. Abraham quickly releases Isaac, and together they disentangle the ram, bind him and place him on the altar. There on the top of the hill, that offering is made in Isaac's place. It dies on the altar *in the stead of his son.* Abraham and Isaac are rejoicing!

The hill of Moriah reminds us of the hill of Calvary. The Lord Jesus took my place; He died in my guilty room and state. I need to contemplate this. I need to climb the

hill of the Cross and learn that my dear Saviour took my
place.

There was One who was willing to die in my stead,
That a soul so unworthy might live;
And the path to the cross He was willing to tread,
All the sins of my life to forgive.

They are nailed to the cross,
They are nailed to the cross,
O how much He was willing to bear!
With what anguish and loss
Jesus went to the cross!
But He carried my sins with Him there.

4. *And Abraham called the name of that place Jehovah-jireh: as it*
    is said to this day, In the mount of the LORD it shall be seen
    (Genesis 22:14). With ecstatic heart and with praise for
    his God, Abraham calls the place *Jehovah-jireh*, meaning,
    the LORD will see, or the LORD will provide. And from that
    day onwards, although Abraham has always loved his
    son—he is his only and dearly loved son—yet from now
    on, since Isaac has been given back to him, as one raised
    from the dead, there's a new value, a new estimate set
    upon Isaac.
    Hebrews 11:17 to 19 enlightens us even further as to
    Abraham's understanding of the Moriah experience, *By*
    faith Abraham, when he was tried, offered up Isaac. . .Accounting
    that God was able to raise him up, even from the dead; from
    whence also he received him in a figure. When the Scripture
    says that Abraham *received him in a figure*, it teaches us
    that Abraham here understands the purpose of God in
    sending him to Moriah is not purely hardship. It is not
    purely testing in anguish of soul and a crisis of faith. Oh it
    is that, but God has had a greater purpose in sending him
    to Moriah! Far more than a difficult test, Moriah is joy—
    glorious, unbounded joy—for the Lord is giving him a

glimpse of Jesus on that hillside. The Lord is showing him Calvary. He has received Isaac *in a figure*. This means he sees that Isaac is a type of Christ! He prefigures the One Who will come in our place. He understands that everything in this incredible journey has had a wonderful purpose. He could not see it before, but now the veil has been lifted, and he sees clearly. He understands the sacrifice of Christ, the message of the Cross. He sees it so much so, that the New Testament declares in John 8:56, *Your father Abraham rejoiced to see my day: and he saw it, and was glad.* Abraham sees Christ's day there at the northernmost summit of Moriah, the place that later will be called Calvary. There, centuries ahead of time, where a father takes his only beloved son and offers him up, God is depicting forever the great act of redemption to come, many, many years in the future.

The blessed work of the Lord Jesus upon the cross is both to be seen by the eye of faith and proclaimed in song and word by every child of God.

What is the result of that amazing scene enacted on the top of Mount Moriah? One small phrase in Genesis 22, verse 14, tells us: *And Abraham called the name of that place Jehovah-jireh: as it is said to this day, In the mount of the LORD it shall be seen.* The meaning of Mount Moriah, the meaning of *Jehovah-jireh* refers to what the Lord has provided. "It shall be seen how the Lord made the provision of the lamb. And it is talked about to this day!" *It is said to this day.* If that means anything, it means that the circumstances recorded here in Genesis 22 become the focus of discussion among God's people. In the centuries to follow, God's people are still talking about the Mount Moriah scene. It is the theme of their conversation, the focus of their interest. Not just casually, not just once in a while, *but as it is said to this day,* they're still talking about it! And what is the theme of the Bible? What is the theme of the song of Heaven? "Worthy is the Lamb that was slain." The theme of Heaven is the great act of redemption, the work performed by Jesus Christ, God's dear Son, on Calvary's hill. *As it is said to this day*, we still talk about the Cross. We can't get away from the Gospel. The theme for the Christian is not first of all good works, or the need of the world. These are all good themes, but we must speak of the Cross. We must also sing of Him. The message of the Bible is Jesus Christ and Him crucified, *as it is said to this day*.

> *My song is love unknown,*
> *My Saviour's love to me,*
> *Love to the loveless shown,*
> *That they might lovely be.*
> *Oh who am I,*
> *That for my sake*
> *My Lord should take*
> *Frail flesh, and die?*
>
> *Here might I stay and sing,*
> *No story so divine;*
> *Never was love, dear King,*
> *Never was grief like Thine.*
> *This is my Friend,*
> *In whose sweet praise*
> *I all my days*
> *Could gladly spend.*

Moriah—let us gaze at this scene. Let us not turn away to descend the hill too soon. The Lord has much to teach us here. Two great themes have occupied our thoughts: the Lamb of God sacrificed for His people, and God's testing in the life of every child of His. Perhaps the Lord is testing *you*, Christian friend. Are you prepared to give up your Isaac to put the Lord Jesus in first place? What are you going to do in the time of trial? You may be saying, "I could never have done what Abraham did. I must be honest and say that I could not rise to that height of discipleship. I am not an equal to Abraham."

Nevertheless, the record is here for you to learn about the Christian in trial.

The story is told of young D. L. Moody who, during a visit to Britain, found himself sitting in a Dublin city park with the English preacher, Henry Varley. Deep in conversation with Mr. Varley, Moody was suddenly struck by the older preacher's statement, "The world has yet to see what God can do with and for and through and in a man who is fully and wholly consecrated to Him." That spoken word reached to the depths of his soul, and later Mr. Moody recounted that as he thought over the words, he vowed in his heart, "By the grace of God, I'll be that man." Certainly the world did witness how God used a man wholly surrendered to Him. If you mean to understand what it is to submit yourself to God, to submit yourself to His will, to yield all to Him, you need to think on the lessons of Genesis 22. Has not God revealed to us here the height and depth and breadth of His love? Can we not leave all to follow such a Saviour? Will we hold on to the things of time and sense in the time of testing?

The Christian in trial—to what *should* he cling? To what do we find Abraham clinging? Does not Abraham constantly remember the covenant? He remembers the Word of God to him. He rests on the promise. Let us also take to ourselves the special promises and comforts that God has given to us in His Word.

Why the Lord in His unfailing love and faithfulness to His saints allows the times of chastening to come.

First, we see that Abraham's test has a definite, eternal purpose. It is not a miserable experience in a meaningless vacuum. We can say with certainty that **God has a definite purpose for every trial that comes into the life of the Christian.** No matter how many afflictions the Christian is led to pass through, he should fix his mind on this, that God will cause all these things to work out for his advantage. *And we know that **all things** work together for **good** to them that love*

God, to them who are the called according to his purpose (Romans 8:28). Perhaps your trial is that particularly bitter one in which you have been asked to endure the deliberate ill will of someone's hostility. It is a difficult trial in which somebody means to do you harm. Joseph, you remember, experienced such a test; but he testifies to us in Genesis 50, verse 20, that even then, God had a purpose: *But as for you, ye thought evil against me; but God meant it unto good, to bring to pass, as it is this day, to save much people alive.* Here I learn that, in spite of the intentions of men, God will cause the trials that come our way—even those things that others intend for evil—to work out for good. God is always on the throne, and He always remembers His own. So then, the Lord's purpose prevails. People may intend wickedness and hurt, but Joseph says the Lord overrules it all and works it out for good.

Further, we see that Abraham's test is tempered, and in line with his maturity and understanding. He is not given a trial beyond the grace that God has wrought in him. There is a remarkable verse in I Corinthians 10 verse 13: *There hath no temptation taken you but such as is common to man: but God is faithful, who will not suffer you to be tempted above that ye are able; but will with the temptation also make a way to escape, that ye may be able to bear it.* This tells us that **the Lord will temper all our adversities**. He will see to it that no trial will ever come the way of His child, but that which is within his capabilities. These trials are common to man. You may say, "I don't know anybody else afflicted as I am. I don't know anybody else who has had the trials and the disappointments, who has shed the tears that I have had to shed." Child of God, contemplate Moriah. Consider Calvary. Know that God is a faithful God, a loving God, Whose love led the Saviour to Golgotha's hill. These trials are common to man. The Lord knows your frame. He knows what you can bear. He is taking care of you. And He will have His hand also on the knob that controls the heat of the furnace. *He will not suffer you to be tempted above that ye are able.*

Finally, we see that Abraham's test requires that he give over to the Lord everything in regard to that trial. Abraham does not have to manage every detail. He knows God will see to it that the covenant is taken care of, that the line to the blessing will not be destroyed. He understands that God is able to do all things well. His part is to trust and obey. I Peter 4:19 says it this way: *Wherefore let them that suffer according to the will of God commit the keeping of their souls to him in well doing, as unto a faithful Creator.* **God asks only one thing of us in every trial—simple trust and obedience.** Don't be letting affliction lead you to do wrong. Don't be letting hurt that you have suffered engender spite. That's going down the wrong track. You're being foolish and wicked in that case, and you'll pay the penalty. Rather, you're to commit the keeping of your soul to Him. Just hand the whole matter over to the Lord. Go into your room. Close the door. Even if the tears course down your cheeks, open the Book! In fact, I Peter 4:19 would be a good place to start. Declare in submission, "If I'm going to suffer according to the will of God, then let me commit the keeping of my soul, the directing of my life, into His hands. Let me ask the Lord to take control of it all, and to take control of the others, even some who mean to do me harm. Let me give the whole thing to Him."

Listen, child of God, the Lord is your faithful Creator. He brought you into this world, and He did it to make you a child of His love! He did not create you to make you miserable. He brought you into this world to show forth the grace and the goodness of the Lord in your life! And, praise His name, the Lord's well able to look after you. He has looked after you all these years. God tells us unequivocally in Hebrews 12 that if chastening comes to the Christian, it is for his profit. We're told that, although for the present it may bring tears and grief, afterwards it yields the peaceable fruit of righteousness. So I know then, my Saviour doeth all things well. Learn this lesson well, for you may have to walk alone tomorrow. You may have tears tomorrow. You may have a hard road to go next year. You will come to a test; and I know, my Christian friend, that

if you give your life to Him, and your sorrows to Him, and
your worries to Him, the Lord will keep things in His hands.
And at the end of the day, you will say, "My Jesus has done all
things well. He has not given me more than I can bear. He has
walked with me through the trial, He has been faithful, and
He has demonstrated a holy, eternal purpose in it all that has
far outweighed the test. I have learned to trust Him as never
before."

Abraham turns away from Moriah's altar and prepares to
descend the hill with Isaac. But the Holy Spirit records one
more detail in this account. Genesis 22, verses 15 to 18: And
the angel of the LORD called unto Abraham out of heaven the
second time, And said, By myself have I sworn, saith the
LORD, for because thou hast done this thing, and hast not
withheld thy son, thine only son: That in blessing I will bless
thee, and in multiplying I will multiply thy seed as the stars
of the heaven, and as the sand which is upon the sea shore;
and thy seed shall possess the gate of his enemies; And in thy
seed shall all the nations of the earth be blessed; because thou
hast obeyed my voice. Certainly, this final blessing reminds
us that the Lord has been with Abraham every step of this
test. He has seen all. He has directed everything. And look at
the blessing that has come to Abraham. He has come out of
the test far better than he went into it. The testing hasn't
worked against him; it has been for his profit. Only the Lord
can do that! Does Abraham regret going to Moriah? Does he
wish that he had not obeyed God? Never! The last verse of
this story reads simply, *So Abraham returned unto his young men,*
and they rose up and went together to Beer-sheba; and Abraham
dwelt at Beer-sheba. Ah, but what is he doing as he returns
from Moriah? The Scripture doesn't need to spell it out.
Abraham is rejoicing! He comes down that hillside glad that
he has obeyed the Lord, thankful that he has followed the Lord.
He has proved the Lord to be faithful. He has received a
blessing that will go on and on and on. He has seen Calvary.
Your father Abraham rejoiced to see my day: and he saw it, and was
glad. **You will never have any regrets in following the Lord.**

And when you put your life in His hands, you can say, *All things work together for* **good.**

> *King of my life, I crown Thee now,*
> *Thine shall the glory be;*
> *Lest I forget Thy thorn-crowned brow,*
> *Lead me to Calvary.*

> *May I be willing, Lord, to bear*
> *Daily my cross for Thee;*
> *Even Thy cup of grief to share,*
> *Thou hast borne all for me.*

I believe that only those who know the Lord can really climb the hill of Calvary. The Scripture asks the question, *Is it nothing to you, all ye that pass by?* If you've never been to the Cross with a broken heart, if you have never been to the Cross with thoughts of contemplating there what the Lord has done for you, then you do not know the Lamb of Calvary Whose blood can wash away your sin. You are yet separated from God. You must gaze on the sacrifice as Abraham looked. And how he must have looked, for he saw the offering God had provided in the place of his son. His son would live because of the sacrifice made in his stead. Calvary meant something to Abraham. It would ever mean pardon and life and indescribable love. Calvary should mean something to you. Have you ever thought about the death of Christ? Have you ever thought of what the Lord gave up for His people? Have you considered the great wickedness of your sin? Have you ever considered that if you don't run to the Cross, if you don't have the blood of Christ applied to your heart, you'll have His blood under your feet? You will trample underfoot the blood of the Lord Jesus Christ on your way to hell. It is necessary for us to linger at the hill of the Cross. We need the Lord's mercy more than we need anything else. Think about the Lamb. Think about the meaning of the Cross for you.

O teach me what it meaneth;
That cross uplifted high,
With One, the Man of Sorrows,
Condemned to bleed and die.
O teach me what it cost Thee
To make a sinner whole;
And teach me, Saviour, teach me
The value of a soul.

O teach me what it meaneth;
That sacred crimson tide,
The blood and water flowing
From Thine own wounded side.
Teach me that if none other
Had sinned, but I alone,
Yet still, Thy Blood, Lord Jesus
Thine only, must atone.

O teach me what it meaneth;
For I am full of sin;
And grace alone can reach me,
And love alone can win.
O teach me, for I need Thee,
I have no hope beside,
The chief of all the sinners
For whom the Saviour died.

Lord we need Thee. Put Thy hand upon us. Come and stay every
thought that would in some way get between us and Thee. May Thy
Holy Spirit prevail with us. Do not let us leave this study careless—
careless about our sins, careless about the state of our souls, careless
about eternity. Oh God, speak. Defeat every purpose of the devil.
Bring the will of our flesh to nothing. We pray that the allurement
of the world will be as nothing. May our eyes be filled with the glory
of God. May our hearts be taken up with Jesus Christ and Him
crucified. May we learn the meaning of the Cross. May we learn
what it meant to Thee, the Holy One, to bear away our sins. May

our hearts be moved. Help us to follow in the footsteps of Abraham as disciples of the Lord Jesus Christ. May our lives be changed. May they become a praise to Thee. Cause Thy Word to prosper in the thing whereto Thou hast sent it. Abide with us now. We thank Thee. In Jesus' name, amen.